The
Parables
— of the —
Qur'an

DR YASIR QADHI

KUBE
PUBLISHING

The Parables of the Qur'an

First published in England by
Kube Publishing Ltd
Markfield Conference Centre
Ratby Lane, Markfield
Leicestershire, LE67 9SY
United Kingdom

Tel: +44 (0) 1530 249230

Email: info@ kubepublishing.com
Website: www.kubepublishing.com

ISBN: 978-1-84774-179-0 casebound
ISBN: 978-1-84774-180-6 ebook

Editor: Wordsmiths
Cover design, Arabic calligraphy and typesetting by: Jannah Haque
Printed by: IMAK, Turkey

Transliteration

A brief guide to some of the letters and symbols used in the Arabic transliteration in this book.

th	ث	*ḥ*	ح	*dh*	ذ
ṣ	ص	*ḍ*	ض	*ṭ*	ط
ẓ	ظ	ʿ	ع	ʾ	ء

ā	◌َا ◌َ	*ī*	◌ِي	*ū*	◌ُو

May the peace and
blessings of Allah
be upon him.

May Allah
be pleased
with him.

May Allah
be pleased
with her.

May Allah be pleased
with them both.

May He
be glorified.

May peace be
upon him.

Contents

Section Two: Aphorisms

Preface

All praise is due to Allah, and may salutations be upon the Messenger of Allah!

Every Ramadan for the last decade, it has been my habit to undertake a lecture series for my *masjid* that aims to both uplift the *īmān* of the attendees and provide wholesome spiritual benefit. Last year, in Ramadan 1442 AH, I decided to concentrate on some of the parables and aphorisms of the Qur'an. Each day, I would choose a parable or aphorism and explain it to the attendees during the *tarāwīḥ* prayers. This work in your hands is the culmination of that project.

The work begins with a chapter on the eloquence of the Qur'an and the role that parables (*amthāl*) play in it. We discuss what exactly a 'parable' is, the key components of a parable, and why it is so effective. Further, I illustrate the function of the parable in the Qur'an and how Allah references it. I then explain how 'aphorisms' have become so common that it is used as everyday sayings, or expressions of wisdom, by all Arabic speakers regardless of faith.

The work is divided into two sections. In the first section, 25 specific parables are discussed in the order of the Surahs of the Qur'an in which they are mentioned. The goal is to explain these parables in a simple manner without the technical language typically found in advanced works of exegesis. In the second section, a few aphorisms are chosen to illustrate

this phenomenon. Of course, it is difficult to have a comprehensive list, as any Qur'anic phrase can be used in such a manner if one chooses to do so.

I would like to thank Kube Publishing and their editorial staff for working with me so tirelessly to produce such a polished product. Of course, as always, I forever remain grateful to my Lord for blessing me with a loving family. I think of all of the introductions I have written over the last 25 years—for over a dozen books that I have published—I began as a bachelor, thanking my parents; then over the years I also thanked my wife; and one by one, my children were added to the list. Now to see that my 'children' are young adults, and my elderly parents have moved in with me, I can only say, as the Qur'an instructs,

"My Lord! Inspire me to ever be thankful for Your favours which You blessed me and my parents with, and to do good deeds that please You. And instill righteousness in my offspring. I truly repent to You, and I truly submit to Your Will." [1]

Dr. Yasir Qadhi
Plano, TX
January 30th, 2022 CE
(Jumādā al-Ākhirah 27th, 1443 AH)

---

[1] *Al-Aḥqāf*, 15.

وَتِلْكَ الْأَمْثَلُ

نَضْرِبُهَا لِلنَّاسِ

وَمَا يَعْقِلُهَا

إِلَّا الْعَلِمُونَ

These are the parables that we cite
for mankind, and it is only those
who ponder and understand that
benefit from the parables.

AL-ʿANKABŪT, 43.

INTRODUCTION

Figures of Speech in the Qur'an:
The Use of Symbolism and Imagery

There can be no doubt that the most honoured, revered, and eloquent of all speech is the speech of our Creator, Allah 🕮. Furthermore, Allah 🕮 honoured us immensely by selecting us to be the recipients of such noble speech, in the form of the Qur'an that was revealed to our beloved Messenger 🕮. This Qur'an holds great power as well as the ability to reform, rectify, and revolutionalise through its eloquent presentations. Part of this unparalleled eloquence is its impressive use of various linguistic mechanisms and rhetorical devices to beautifully convey its message. Facts are wonderfully presented, as well as striking themes of *targhīb* (inspiring) and *tarhīb* (warning) that incentivise us, push us to yearn and desire, and certainly fear those things that Allah 🕮 wishes for us to fear. Another powerful mechanism employed in the Qur'an is the presentation of stories and examples in order to convey distinct facts and remarkable messages. In fact, these are some of the Qur'an's most effective mechanisms, known as *amthāl* (parables).

Regarding this, Allah 🕮 says in the Noble Qur'an,

وَتِلْكَ الْأَمْثَالُ نَضْرِبُهَا لِلنَّاسِ، وَمَا يَعْقِلُهَا إِلَّا الْعَالِمُونَ

"These are the parables that we cite for mankind, and it is only those who ponder and understand that benefit from the parables." [2]

2

---

[2] *Al-'Ankabūt*, 43.

Further adding to this, Allah ﷻ says,

وَلَقَدْ ضَرَبْنَا لِلنَّاسِ فِي هَٰذَا الْقُرْآنِ مِن كُلِّ مَثَلٍ لَّعَلَّهُمْ يَتَذَكَّرُونَ

"We have cited every type of parable in this Qur'an so that they can understand and think." [3]

In another verse, Allah ﷻ says,

وَتِلْكَ الْأَمْثَالُ نَضْرِبُهَا لِلنَّاسِ لَعَلَّهُمْ يَتَفَكَّرُونَ

"These are the parables we cite for mankind so that they can benefit and ponder." [4]

Thus, we clearly understand from these verses that the purpose of the divine revelation of this Noble Book is for us to ponder, reflect, and benefit from its insightful wisdoms. To facilitate this, Allah ﷻ has placed within the Qur'an numerous parables that aid us in fulfilling these lofty aims. Another astounding quality of this linguistic mechanism is that upon surveying the parables found in the Qur'an, we will find not just one category of parables, but multiform parables of various categories.

Among these, the first category of Qur'anic parable is the chronicle—a non-fictitious historic parable which Allah ﷻ

---

[3] *Al-Zumar*, 27.

[4] *Al-Ḥashr*, 21.

instructs us to keenly deliberate upon. Doing so will allow us to derive lessons, inspiration, and life-reforming benefits from the divine speech and the chronicled incidents contained therein. A brilliant example of this is the powerful chronicle of the two gardens found in *Sūrah al-Kahf*—a chronicle that certainly strikes any attentive reader. This chronicle is not fiction, but a bona fide historical occurrence.

Elsewhere, Allah ﷻ mentions in *Sūrah Yā Sīn*,

$$وَاضْرِبْ لَهُم مَّثَلًا أَصْحَابَ الْقَرْيَةِ$$

"Cite for them the parable of the people of the village."[5]

The '*qaryah* (village)' mentioned in this verse refers to the ancient village of Antioch (أَنْطَاكِيَة). The chronicle being presented in this passage of the Qur'an is completely genuine. Thus, chronicles are a powerful type of Qur'anic parable; they are worthy of being discussed in much more detail, for certainly they are an enlightening area of discourse. However, for the purposes of this work, these few examples will have to suffice, as this type of historic parable is not the topic of our discourse.

The focus of our discourse will be around a second category of parables—the parables that employ symbolism. Symbolism refers to the Qur'an's usage of language that creates imagery in

---

[5] *Yā Sīn*, 13.

relation to any natural object or creature. For example, in one verse of the Qur'an, Allah ﷻ makes mention of a mosquito. This is a form of imagery. In another verse, the Qur'an also mentions an ant. Allah ﷻ also makes mention of the opposing concepts of light and darkness, using these terms to demonstrate the likeness of an individual who has true vision in contrast with one who does not. Allah ﷻ constantly uses images that the common person is cognisant of and then utilises that same image to emphasise a striking message in relation to something He wishes for us to comprehend. Furthermore, the imagery utilised by Allah ﷻ is not standard imagery, but imagery of an astoundingly vivid nature. From such staggering imagery, Allah ﷻ extracts potent lessons for us. This wonderful topic will be the subject of our discourse, *in shā' Allāh*.

Moving ahead, our discourse will be centred around three core components found in all symbolic parables. These three components can be found and extracted from the following verse of the Noble Qur'an,

مَثَلُ الَّذِينَ يُنْفِقُونَ أَمْوَالَهُمْ فِي سَبِيلِ اللَّهِ كَمَثَلِ حَبَّةٍ أَنْبَتَتْ سَبْعَ سَنَابِلَ فِي كُلِّ سُنْبُلَةٍ مِائَةُ حَبَّةٍ

"He who spends his wealth for the sake of Allah is like the one who plants a seed, that one seed gives seven corn ears, every one of those seven gives one hundred grains."[6]

---

[6] *Al-Baqarah*, 261.

The three components that every symbolic parable must be comprised of are:

The actual imagery—in this particular example, the seed giving seven corn ears, and the seven corn ears having one hundred seeds within them.

The purpose of the presentation of this particular imagery in the way it has been presented.

The commonality factor—exploring what exactly links the image and the cause. In the example of this parable, the commonality factor is rapid and large multiplication, eventually resulting in a plethora not possessed previously. This is found in the imagery of one seed multiplying to potentially become 700 seeds.

We can see from this verse and the various other verses containing symbolic parables that this subject is exceedingly wonderful and pleasing to discuss. Due to this, in our tradition, the scholars have paid special attention to this theme by including discussions on it in their works. In the field of *'Ulūm al-Qur'an* (sciences of the Qur'an), we will find that every comprehensive work contains a discussion on it. The renowned scholar Ibn Qayyim al-Jawziyyah ﷺ penned an entire treatise titled *Amthāl al-Qur'an*. Imam al-Zarkashī ﷺ authored a celebrated and famed encyclopedia, in which he comprehensively discusses all aspects related to the Qur'an. In this seminal work, the Imam has dedicated an

entire chapter to the subject of parables of the Qur'an. The eponymous founder of the Shāfiʿī school, Imam al-Shāfiʿī ﷺ once stated that it is not permitted for an individual to attempt interpreting the Qur'an until he comprehends the subject of the parables of the Qur'an. These are all examples of the great attention the scholars of this nation paid to this subject. This emphasis is because they recognised the importance and power of the parables of the Qur'an.

Another related topic is Qur'anic aphorisms—those phrases that have become symbolic in Arab linguistic culture, and used as revered statements of utmost wisdom. Along with parables, these are also exceedingly powerful. This is not denying that the entire Qur'an is powerful, but there are certain linguistic mechanisms that are exceedingly powerful and vivid to the reader, such that they have found their way into becoming part of the vernacular of societies and civilisations.

Based on these facts, in our discourse, we intend to discuss many of the Qur'anic parables and aphorisms, *in shā' Allāh*. We will not be able to cover their entirety due to the sheer number of them, for there are perhaps thousands of actual aphorisms in the Qur'an and dozens of parables. The goal of this work is not to be comprehensive, but to introduce a fair amount and achieve a suitable target for us to become acquainted with this topic and concept, *in shā' Allāh*.

وَلَقَدْ ضَرَبْنَا لِلنَّاسِ

فِى هَٰذَا الْقُرْآنِ

مِن كُلِّ مَثَلٍ

لَعَلَّهُمْ يَتَذَكَّرُونَ

We have cited every type of
parable in this Qur'an so that they
can understand and think.

AL-ZUMAR, 27.

SECTION ONE

Parables

1

The Danger of Hypocrisy:
The Parable of Fire and Light

In the Qur'an, Allah ﷻ primarily categorises humankind into three groups. We find this categorisation in the striking opening verses of *Sūrah al-Baqarah*, where Allah first describes the sincere believers in five wonderful verses. Next, Allah ﷻ describes the *kuffār* (disbelievers) in two verses, which is then immediately followed by thirteen comprehensive verses meticulously describing the hypocrites.

This phenomenon of *nifāq* (hypocrisy) is an abstract concept to those living in lands of disbelief. Therefore, most people fail to fully comprehend this concept due to a lack of interaction with obvious hypocrites. This is because, in such lands, since Muslims are in a minority situation with no worldly benefits of being visibly Muslim, the frequent visitation of the houses of Allah, coupled with the general religious effort of those professing adherence to the Islamic faith, is considered to be a true measure of the quality of a person's faith. In such circumstances, this is certainly a good measure of sincerity!

However, an important concept for us to grasp is that when Islam becomes a state religion with political dominance, the door to hypocrisy flings wide open. In such circumstances, you will discover individuals that do not hold sincere faith and belief within their hearts, yet they outwardly exhibit exemplary behaviour identical to the behaviour of sincere believers. They do this in order to attain the societal benefits of identifying as believers. For a living example of this, we need to look no further than the events that immediately followed the tragic incident that took place in New York on 11 September 2001 (9/11). After the horrific attacks, certain nefarious individuals hoping to mitigate the backlash against themselves—taken as 'token Muslims'—would appear on satellite stations such as Fox News, spurting vile conjecture, levelling spurious accusations, and engaging in uncalled for criticism of our own people. It is as if these wicked individuals—people being presented as 'Imams' or 'community leaders'—were attempting to distance themselves from people of their own skin colour and background. They were singing to the tune of the narrative of biased media channels that had dedicated themselves to hate-mongering. Such foolish individuals, with the intention of obtaining the meagre provisions and security of the *dunyā*, are selling themselves out, and in the process damning themselves in the Hereafter. They made

an unprofitable trade, exchanging their *dīn* for the *dunyā*. What a foolish trade!

This is a prime example of the phenomenon of *nifāq*, and perhaps the closest we will get in our times to seeing that reality.

In *Sūrah al-Baqarah*, Allah ﷻ says regarding the hypocrites,

مَثَلُهُمْ كَمَثَلِ الَّذِى اسْتَوْقَدَ نَارًا فَلَمَّا أَضَاءَتْ مَا حَوْلَهُ ذَهَبَ اللهُ بِنُورِهِمْ وَتَرَكَهُمْ فِى ظُلُمَاتٍ لَّا يُبْصِرُونَ

"Their example is that of someone who kindles a fire, but when it lights up all around them, Allah takes away their light, leaving them in complete darkness—unable to see."[7]

In this verse, Allah ﷻ presents an example to us that refers to those hypocrites who profit from the benefits of outwardly exhibiting Islam, yet their internal state is that of arrogant refusal and sheer disbelief. They only exhibit belief for the political and social advantages of doing so. Allah ﷻ provides their example by comparing them to an individual not possessing light nor fire, who asks someone to kindle a fire for them. They appeal to the true believers and to the Prophet ﷺ, seeking *hidāyah* (guidance) by means of an illuminating light that emanates from a bright fire. They originally possess a minimal amount of good within them;

---

[7] *Al-Baqarah*, 17.

hence they make this appeal for a fire to be kindled for them. However, once that fire has been kindled, their surroundings have been illuminated, and they can momentarily see, that illuminating light is snatched away from them, leaving them wandering aimlessly in the dark.

The illuminating light (*nūr*) mentioned in this verse is actually a metaphor. In reality, it refers to the incredible guidance found within the Qur'an that Allah endows His selected slaves with. Allah ﷻ has utilised the metaphor of light to define His guidance, and that of darkness to define misguidance. Furthermore, *al-Nūr* ('The Light') is one of the beautiful names of Allah, a description of the Qur'an, and one of the descriptive titles of the Prophet ﷺ—as found in a verse of the Qur'an.

As for the hypocrite, he is an individual devoid of any enlightening guidance. His situation is so despicable and lowly. Even after witnessing the light of the sincere believers—that he can easily walk within in order to secure his own path of illuminated life—he remains arrogant and chooses to continue wandering in darkness. Such foolish individuals approach the sincere believers, hypocritically requesting them to show them the guidance of Islam. In goodwill, the sincere and unselfish believer provides wonderful explanations of Islam, thus illuminating their surroundings and allowing all those who wish to benefit from this light to receive it without reproach or harm. This unselfishness is the defining quality of a sincere believer, showing us the unshakable strength of the sincere believer's faith. The sincere believer emanates darkness-dispelling light through these efforts; such light can be used for others to gain guidance by the permission of Allah. Despite all these efforts and the spread of plentiful light, the foolish hypocrite makes a conscious decision to ignore the guiding light, while fully understanding the need for it. This is the disastrous result of his arrogance.

This then begs the question of why these hypocrites choose to behave with such foolish and damning arrogance. Upon surveying the situation and circumstances, a few possibilities present themselves. The most prominent of these is the hypocrite's feeling of arrogant dismay at not being personally selected to be the original recipient of the religion. Historically, this was the primary factor behind the hypocrisy of the proud amongst the people of Madinah, who questioned the reason why the Quraysh were the first recipients of the prophetic call.

Allah ﷻ then seals the hearts of such arrogant individuals, who reject the light after having witnessed its guiding power. Allah snatches their spiritual insight away from them, for such damned individuals did not benefit from the guiding light of Allah nor were they worthy of even seeing light in the future. This does not mean that the light of Islam itself is extinguished; rather the light is still shining in all its former glory—only that the hypocrite will be unable to sense it.

Allah ﷻ provides a symbolic parable in the Qur'an in regard to this snatching of light. Allah ﷻ says that the hypocrites will see the believers on the Day of Judgment, walking with the light of their faith towards Paradise.

Upon this, the hypocrite will say,

انظُرُونَا نَقْتَبِسْ مِن نُّورِكُمْ

"Let us seek guidance from your light." [8]

Allah will then inform them that they will not be able to benefit from the light of the sincere believers on that Day, in the same way that they did not benefit from their light in the *dunyā*.

Allah ﷻ also says,

ذَهَبَ اللهُ بِنُورِهِمْ وَتَرَكَهُمْ فِى ظُلُمَٰتٍ لَّا يُبْصِرُونَ

"Allah shall leave them in the plural of darkness, not just one darkness but multiple layers of darkness." [9]

Thus, Allah will abandon them and not pay attention to them again.

---

[8] *Al-Ḥadīd*, 13.

[9] *Al-Baqarah*, 17.

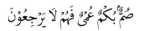

صُمٌّ بُكْمٌ عُمْيٌ فَهُمْ لَا يَرْجِعُونَ

"Deaf, dumb, and blind, they shall not return." [10]

All glory be to Allah. This is a Qur'anic metaphor in relation to the arrogant state of the hypocrites, describing how Allah ﷻ snatches away their spiritual faculties, leaving them unable to sense and perceive the apparent light of guidance after their initial refusal. Their [spiritual] hearts have been sealed from perceiving the truth. Their [spiritual] ears have been sealed from hearing the guidance. Their [spiritual] eyes have become blind from the light of guidance. The Qur'an uses the metaphor of 'deaf, dumb, and blind' to refer to their spiritual loss of faculties; if a physically deaf, dumb, and blind person is left alone in the middle of a barren and isolated desert, how will he find any guidance and salvation? Similarly, the hypocrites can physically see the world but spiritually they are deaf, dumb, and blind; damning themselves through their arrogance and never returning to the right path. This is despite the light that is shining brightly for all to benefit from, but it is they themselves who refuse to take advantage of that guiding light.

In our current circumstances, we are not overly concerned about *al-nifāq al-akbar* (greater hypocrisy) in Islam. Regular attendance of the *masājid* as well as exhibiting righteous and pious behaviour is a good sign of a person's faith, but what

THE PARABLES OF THE QUR'AN

---

[10] *Al-Baqarah*, 18.

we really need to be concerned about is minor hypocrisy—knowing and recognising the truth yet blatantly ignoring it, even partially. This is also a type of hypocrisy. We must take utmost care not to fall into this, ensuring that we recognise, affirm, and follow the truth. If we do not do so, we open the doors to minor hypocrisy upon us. We ask Allah ﷻ to bless us with the divine enablement to see the truth, recognise the truth, and always follow the truth along with those who affirm it.

2

A Warning for the Hypocrites:
The Parable
of the Rainstorm

In the previous chapter, we examined the first parable found in *Sūrah al-Baqarah*, in which the hypocrites are discussed. In order to enhance the discussion, in verse seventeen, Allah ﷻ uses the parable of the fire that they requested to be kindled. Immediately afterwards, in verse nineteen, Allah ﷻ continues discussing the theme of hypocrisy using a parable related to water. There is a potent form of imagery here in relation to fire and water being linked in back-to-back parables.

أَوْ كَصَيِّبٍ مِّنَ السَّمَاءِ

"Or [it is] like a rainstorm from the sky" [11]

---

[11] *Al-Baqarah*, 19.

This particular parable also relates to the hypocrites; however, the specific category of hypocrites being referred to is not identical to the previously mentioned hypocrites cited in the verse,

صُمٌّ بُكْمٌ عُمْيٌ فَهُمْ لَا يَرْجِعُونَ

"Deaf, dumb, and blind—so they will not return [to the right path]."[12]

These deaf, dumb, and blind individuals were the notorious leaders of the hypocrites, such as 'Abdullāh ibn Ubayy ibn Salūl. They were those criminals that had recognised the truth, yet they stubbornly turned their backs and refused to come to a sincere expression of Islam. However, along with these individuals, there was another category of hypocrites, regarding whom Allāh ﷻ says,

مُّذَبْذَبِينَ بَيْنَ ذَٰلِكَ لَا إِلَىٰ هَٰؤُلَاءِ وَلَا إِلَىٰ هَٰؤُلَاءِ

"Torn between belief and disbelief—belonging neither to these [believers] nor those [disbelievers]."[13]

These hypocrites were those who were sometimes close to sincerely accepting Islam, and at other times stubbornly clinging to arrogant disbelief. In relation to this second

---

[12] *Al-Baqarah*, 18.

[13] *Al-Nisā'*, 143.

category, Allah ﷻ also mentions in the Qur'an that there are hypocrites around Madinah; you do not know who they are, but Allah certainly knows them. The evil of this category of hypocrites is lesser than the first category. This is as their occasional inclination to Islam evidences some degree of good within them, despite the fact that they are yet to sincerely believe. The parable in the following verse is in relation to such people,

أَوْ كَصَيِّبٍ مِّنَ السَّمَاءِ

"Or [it is] like a rainstorm from the sky" [14]

In this parable, by way of example, the hypocrites are likened to a group of people who are lost in a desolate desert. Whilst they are in this dire predicament, suddenly heavy rain descends from the heavens, and they are blessed with much needed water. Any person in such a predicament would welcome such rain, as is the norm amongst Bedouin desert dwellers.

In this wonderful parable, the abundant rains signify and symbolise Islam. Our Prophet ﷺ said, "The example of that which Allah ﷺ has sent me with is like that of rain that descends on groups of people." [15]

[14] *Al-Baqarah*, 19.

[15] *Ṣaḥīḥ Muslim*.

Upon receiving this wonderful rain from the heavens [symbolising Islam], the soil [symbolising the heart of the righteous believers] is fertile and absorbs the rain plentifully, whilst also welcoming it. As for those who stubbornly reject Allah ﷻ and are devoid of faith, their soil is dense and unabsorbing. Thus, they do not benefit from the abundant rain, rejecting the obvious good and choosing to look only at what they perceive as negatives.

Thus, Allah ﷻ continues the verse by saying,

$$\text{فِيهِ ظُلُمَاتٌ وَرَعْدٌ وَبَرْقٌ}$$

"[a rainstorm from the sky] with darkness,
thunder, and lightning." [16]

When this rain descends upon them, they do not reflect on the merciful nature of the water. Rather, they completely neglect its benefits and focus only on the *ẓulumāt* (darkness) that accompanies it. This is a symbol for the hypocrites being overcome by the *ẓulumāt* [symbolising the darkened oppression] of their souls—illicit desires and disbelief. As for the thunder (*ra'd*) and lightning (*barq*), they symbolise the Qur'anic warnings and threats to the disbelievers and hypocrites. The thunder and lightning are from the manifest evidences that the Qur'an is certainly a divinely revealed scripture from Allah ﷻ. Despite this, even after clearly

---

[16] Ibid.

hearing and seeing these signs and verses, the hypocrites remain terrified and refuse to take heed. Their reactions are described by Allah ﷻ,

$$\text{يَجْعَلُونَ أَصَابِعَهُمْ فِي آذَانِهِم مِّنَ الصَّوَاعِقِ حَذَرَ الْمَوْتِ}$$

"They press their fingers into their ears at the sound of every thunder-clap for fear of death." [17]

They press their fingers into their ears in order to block out the message, fearing that accepting the Qur'anic message and Islam might result in them being compelled to give up their frivolous lifestyles. This is so difficult for the hypocrites that they regard it as death. Because they are powerless to stop the descension of the divine rains of truth itself, they instead press their fingers into their ears in order to drown out the sound of the beautiful Qur'anic message that was sent to them. By doing so, they foolishly think that they are protecting themselves from faith. However, this is a mere illusion as they cannot stop the wonderful message from reaching all of mankind. In actual fact, they deprive only themselves by their arrogant behaviour.

[17] Ibid.

Allah ﷻ further says,

$$\text{وَاللَّهُ مُحِيطٌ بِالْكَافِرِينَ}$$

"And Allah encompasses the disbelievers." [18]

Their arrogant behaviour such as the pressing of fingers into their ears will not protect them, for indeed Allah ﷻ will not guide and protect those individuals who do not wish true guidance and protection upon themselves. Instead, He surrounds and encompasses them by His might. In this verse, Allah ﷻ refers to them as '*kāfirīn*' (disbelievers), despite the subject of the verses being the hypocrites (*munāfiqīn*). This is because the hypocrites are the worst type of disbelievers. Regarding the abhorrent hypocrites, Allah ﷻ says,

$$\text{إِنَّ الْمُنَافِقِينَ فِي الدَّرْكِ الْأَسْفَلِ مِنَ النَّارِ}$$

"Surely the hypocrites will be in the lowest depths of the Fire." [19]

---

[18] Ibid.

[19] *Al-Nisā'*, 145.

Allah  further says,

$$\text{يَكَادُ الْبَرْقُ يَخْطَفُ أَبْصَارَهُمْ}$$

"It is as if the lightning were about to
snatch away their sight." [20]

The striking lightning of faith is so clearly visible that they are aware of its reality. It should bedazzle and amaze them, coercing them into submission. However, despite its crystal-clear nature, instead of being amazed and submissive they negatively think that it will blind and harm them.

Allah then says,

$$\text{كُلَّمَا أَضَاءَ لَهُم مَّشَوْا فِيهِ}$$

"Whenever it [the lightning] flashes on them,
they walk in its light." [21]

The affair of these hypocrites is such that whenever they sense some light, they walk a few steps. This symbolises their state when they occasionally do good deeds and exhibit outer faith whilst they are temporarily in the blessed company of the Prophet . However, once this temporary company of the Prophet ends, they turn back on their heels whilst

[20] *Al-Baqarah*, 20.

[21] Ibid.

THE PARABLES OF THE QURAN

renouncing faith and good deeds. An example of this is the difficult circumstances at the Battle of Uḥud, when the tables were turned against the believers during the course of warfare. On occasions such as this, they reveal their true colours and become stagnant, not moving in the light.

$$وَإِذَا أَظْلَمَ عَلَيْهِمْ قَامُوا ۚ وَلَوْ شَاءَ اللَّهُ لَذَهَبَ بِسَمْعِهِمْ وَأَبْصَارِهِمْ ۚ إِنَّ اللَّهَ عَلَىٰ كُلِّ شَيْءٍ قَدِيرٌ$$

"But when darkness covers them, they stand still. Had Allah willed, He could have taken away their hearing and sight. Surely Allah is Most Capable of everything." [22]

We learn from this verse that the second category of hypocrites is not like the first. For Allah ﷻ snatches away the [spiritual] hearing and seeing of the first category, but does not do the same to the second. Allah ﷻ informs us that if He so wishes, He is fully capable of snatching away the hearing and sight of the second category of hypocrites too. However, He intentionally did not, as in His divine knowledge He knew that some amongst them would eventually accept Islam sincerely whilst others would not. This is a reality we know from the Madinan phase.

In summary, this complete metaphor gives us vivid symbolism of faith, disbelief, and hypocrisy. The people of faith appreciate the beneficial rains, thunder, and lightning

---

[22] Ibid

as they are safe and happy in the fortress of sincere faith. On the other hand, the hypocrites who are wandering aimlessly in a desolate desert are unprotected and ill-equipped. Thus, the valuable rain does not benefit them, and the thunder and lightning irritate them. They then make a futile attempt to protect themselves by pressing their fingers in their ears; however, this will not protect them as they have chosen the path of misguidance. Furthermore, if Allah ﷻ so wills, He could punish them more severely, but He grants them some degree of respite due to the fact that some from amongst them eventually embraced Islam.

This vivid metaphor should impress upon us the importance of seeking Allah's ﷻ refuge from major hypocrisy, similar to how we worry about and seek refuge from minor hypocrisy and its signs. We must seek refuge from knowing the truth yet arrogantly refusing to follow it intentionally, metaphorically putting fingers in our ears. This is a dangerous reality. Our hearts must be ever submissive to Allah ﷻ, even if we are not able to show complete dedication through our physical actions. This will ensure we remain far from the boundaries of hypocrisy.

3

Engaging in Remembrance:
A Bidirectional Relationship

In this chapter, we will be exploring a succinct phrase found in *Sūrah al-Baqarah* that only consists of two words but contains much benefit. If we take these words to heart and follow them, they will be sufficient for us all. Allah ﷻ says,

$$فَٱذۡكُرُونِيٓ أَذۡكُرۡكُمۡ$$

"Remember Me; I will remember you."[23]

Allah ﷻ tells us in the first person that if we remember Him, He will remember us. Our remembrance of Allah ﷻ can be of various forms and types. One form of remembrance is prayer (*ṣalāh*). Allah ﷻ says,

---

[23] *Al-Baqarah*, 152.

وَأَقِمِ الصَّلَاةَ لِذِكْرِي

"And establish prayer for My remembrance." [24]

The Qur'an is also a type of remembrance,

إِنَّا نَحْنُ نَزَّلْنَا الذِّكْرَ وَإِنَّا لَهُ لَحَافِظُونَ

"It is certainly We Who have revealed the Reminder,
and it is certainly We Who will preserve it." [25]

This is an addition to the various verbal remembrances (*adhkār*), such as glorification (*tasbīḥ*), praise (*taḥmīd*), proclamation of greatness (*takbīr*), proclamation of oneness (*tahlīl*), and seeking of refuge (*istiʿādhah*). We should constantly engage in all these forms of remembrances, as they have multiple benefits and attract plentiful blessings. These remembrances connect us to Allah ﷻ, cause our forgiveness, elevate our ranks, give life to the heart, uplift our souls, and are the pulse that measures our faith. They remove us from the problems and worries of this world, and are a fortress that protects us from grief and anxiety. They form a wall between us and the Devil. Allah ﷻ will not cast into the Hellfire the tongue that is constantly remembering Him, for our Prophet said that nothing extricates a person from the punishment of Allah ﷻ better than the remembrance of Allah ﷻ.

---

[24] *Ṭā Hā*, 14.

[25] *Al-Ḥijr*, 9.

It is also amazing that remembrance is the one deed that can be performed at any time, place or state, without there being any preconditions. It is an incomparably easy deed that holds blessings beyond our comprehension. A person can be anywhere: standing, sitting, lying down, facing the direction of the *qiblah*, facing another direction, or even experiencing the monthly menstrual cycle. It matters not, as remembrance is a universal form of worship. You can be driving to work, waiting at a traffic light, waiting for a meeting, sitting in a *masjid*, or being at any place—these are all opportunities to remember Allah ﷻ. Our Prophet ﷺ said in a famous Hadith,

كَلِمَتَانِ خَفِيفَتَانِ عَلَى اللِّسَانِ، ثَقِيلَتَانِ فِي الْمِيزَانِ، حَبِيبَتَانِ إِلَى الرَّحْمَنِ، سُبْحَانَ اللهِ وَبِحَمْدِهِ، سُبْحَانَ اللهِ العَظِيمِ

"There are two statements that are dear to the All-Merciful, light upon the tongue, and heavy on the scales: Glory be to Allah and by His praise, Glory be to Allah the Magnificent."

Our Prophet ﷺ also said,

وَالْحَمْدُ لِلَّهِ تَمْلَأُ الْمِيزَانَ

"Alḥamdulillāh fills the scale."

It takes not even a full second to make this remembrance, yet it fills the entire scale with good deeds. What an easy way of attaining immense blessings!

In a beautiful Hadith of Tirmidhī, it is mentioned that an elderly man once came hobbling to the Prophet ﷺ and said:

"O Messenger of Allah! Islam has come to me, and you see my state. I am an old man and I do not have the youth of the other Companions here. I do not have the physical strength to do what most of the other Companions are doing. Therefore, tell me of one deed that I can do at my age that will allow me to reach the level of the others sitting here if I hold firmly onto it."

Our Prophet ﷺ then put his blessed fingers upon his blessed tongue and said,

"Upon you is holding firm onto the remembrance of Allah."

In another Hadith, our Prophet ﷺ said that one's tongue should be constantly moving with the remembrance of Allah ﷻ. In one version of the narration, the man then asked if that was all that was needed to reach the level of the other Companions ﷺ. The Prophet ﷺ replied that you can certainly reach the level of the elite through constant remembrance. This is as remembrance reminds you of Allah ﷻ, which opens the doors to all other good deeds. Thus, as this chapter reaches its conclusion, my advice to myself and all of you is to incorporate remembrance into your life and make it become second nature. Incorporate into your daily routine the sayings of *bismillāh, subḥānallāh, alḥamdulillāh,* and other remembrances. These can be made at any time, such as when you come up your staircase, or as you start your car. If we do so, we will become of those whom Allah  describes as,

وَالذَّاكِرِينَ اللَّهَ كَثِيرًا وَالذَّاكِرَاتِ

"Men and women who remember Allah often." [26]

Allah also says,

يَٰٓأَيُّهَا الَّذِينَ اٰمَنُوا اذْكُرُوا اللَّهَ ذِكْرًا كَثِيرًا۔ وَسَبِّحُوهُ بُكْرَةً وَأَصِيلًا

"O believers! Always remember Allah often and glorify Him in the morning and evening." [27]

I conclude with a beautiful Hadith of our Prophet . On the night he made the miraculous night journey and ascension, he met his ancestor Ibrāhīm , who conveyed to us a sweet and succinct message,

يَا مُحَمَّدُ، أَقْرِئْ أُمَّتَكَ مِنِّي السَّلَامَ

"O Muhammad! Convey to your nation my greetings."

[26] *Al-Aḥzāb,* 35.

[27] *Al-Aḥzāb,* 41-42.

THE PARABLES OF THE QUR'AN

The Prophet Ibrāhīm ﷺ sent his greetings to all of us through his descendant, our Messenger ﷺ himself. He then says,

وَأَخْبِرْهُمْ أَنَّ الْجَنَّةَ طَيِّبَةُ التُّرْبَةِ عَذْبَةُ الْمَاءِ، وَأَنَّهَا قِيعَانٌ وَأَنَّ غِرَاسَهَا سُبْحَانَ اللَّهِ وَالْحَمْدُ لِلَّهِ وَلَا إِلَهَ إِلَّا اللَّهُ وَاللَّهُ أَكْبَرُ

"Inform them that Paradise has a vast plain of pure soil and sweet water, yet it is a plain levelled land. The plants grow there by uttering: subḥānallāh, alḥamdulillāh, lā ilāha illa Allāh, and Allāhu akbar."

The seeds and saplings of Paradise grow through the remembrance of Allah ﷻ. Every time we say *subḥānallāh* a tree is planted, *alḥamdulillāh* leads to the formation of another tree, *Allāhu akbar* forms another tree, and *lā ilāha illa Allāh* brings forth an additional plant. When we remember Allah ﷻ, Allah ﷻ remembers us and takes care of us.

4

Multiplying One's Dividends
in the Hereafter

The next parable in the Qur'an is found in verse 261 of *Sūrah al-Baqarah*, a chapter that was revealed in the Madinan period and encompasses the five pillars of Islam: the testimony of faith, prayer, fasting, almsgiving, and pilgrimage. This makes it one of the few Qur'anic chapters that combine mention of all the pillars of Islam. It is also a chapter that makes mention of the fundamentals of faith as well as various chronicles, and it is no surprise that towards the end of the chapter we find a number of parables. The particular parable we are exploring here is exceedingly simple, sweet, beautiful, and accessible to even a child due to its concise nature. The entire section of the Qur'an in which this parable is found predominantly emphasises giving charity, beginning from the verse preceding the Verse of the Throne (*Āyah al-Kursī*) until the end of *Sūrah al-Baqarah*. Allah ﷻ says,

$$\text{مَّثَلُ الَّذِينَ يُنفِقُونَ أَمْوَالَهُمْ فِي سَبِيلِ اللَّهِ كَمَثَلِ حَبَّةٍ أَنبَتَتْ سَبْعَ سَنَابِلَ فِي كُلِّ سُنبُلَةٍ مِّائَةُ حَبَّةٍ ۗ وَاللَّهُ يُضَاعِفُ لِمَن يَشَاءُ ۗ وَاللَّهُ وَاسِعٌ عَلِيمٌ}$$

"The example of those who spend their wealth in the cause of Allah is that of a grain that sprouts into seven ears, each bearing one hundred grains. And Allah multiplies [the reward even more] to whoever He wills. For Allah is All-Bountiful, All-Knowing." [28]

What an amazing parable! This verse is commonly quoted at fundraising events, due to its inspirational wording and message. Let us now examine in closer detail what makes this verse so inspirational. Allah ﷻ presents to us the parable of the ones who spend their wealth. Allah ﷻ is being generous here by stating 'their wealth', as in reality all wealth belongs to Allah ﷻ alone, and it has only been ascribed to man metaphorically. Allah ﷻ blesses those that He wishes with wealth as a trust, but that wealth still belongs to Him. Allah ﷻ informs us in the Qur'an,

$$\text{وَآتُوهُم مِّن مَّالِ اللَّهِ الَّذِي آتَاكُمْ}$$

"And give them some of Allah's wealth which He has granted you." [29]

28 *Al-Baqarah*, 261.

29 *Al-Nūr*, 33.

From this, we establish that it is Allah's ﷻ wealth. Allah ﷻ also says,

$$\text{أَنفِقُوا مِمَّا جَعَلَكُم مُّسْتَخْلَفِينَ فِيهِ}$$

"Donate from what He [Allah] has entrusted you with." [30]

$$\text{أَنفِقُوا مِمَّا رَزَقْنَاكُم}$$

"Donate from what We [Allah] have provided for you." [31]

Thus, wealth is a trust from Allah, who has delegated this money to us only for a short period of time. Despite this, Allah ﷻ generously says that whoever spends from this wealth and gives a little back to Him (as it is really Allah's ﷻ wealth originally), He gladly accepts that and rewards immensely in recompense.

Demonstrating this, the example of planting a seed that grows, as described in the parable, is very powerful and relevant. It is a metaphor that we can all understand and derive benefits from. We first learn that giving charity is transitive and is, therefore, one of the greatest forms of worship due to the benefit it gives to society. It has been likened to planting seeds. These seeds will eventually sprout and grow into plants that give sweet fruits and flowers, which many people

---

[30] *Al-Ḥadīd*, 7.

[31] *Al-Baqarah*, 254.

THE PARABLES OF THE QURAN

will benefit from. In addition, not only do you benefit those you know, but the notion of helping people in future generations through reoccurring harvests is extremely enriching, and a means of perpetual reward even after your death. Allah knows ﷻ where those plants, flowers, and fruits will grow, who will benefit from their aroma and taste, and where their seeds will then spread to and germinate, thereby producing more plants, fruits, and flowers. This is an ongoing process. Similarly, by sponsoring an orphan, sponsoring someone's education, or giving any other form of charity, you may be benefiting generations of individuals. You could be a means of their quality of life improving even without you knowing or foreseeing the extent of the benefit you were originally a means of.

Another lesson we learn from this parable is that sometimes it takes time before realizing the true benefit of something. In this parable, the seed did not become 700 grains immediately, but went through a process of gradual growth before reaching there. After being planted, it first germinates and grows seven ears, after which 100 grains grow in each ear. Other plants will even grow more grain, which is why Allah ﷻ clarifies, 'and Allah multiplies [the reward even more] to whoever He wills.' Through this example, Allah ﷻ is informing us that we will indeed be generously recompensed when giving for His sake. However, we must first exercise patience and faithfully anticipate the multiplied reward that will certainly come—whether it be multiplied by 700, a lesser amount, or a much higher amount! In a Hadith in the

Musnad of Aḥmad, the Prophet ﷺ is reported to have said that whatever charity you give, you will receive for it ten to seven-hundred rewards in return. This lower limit of 10 is guaranteed, as long as it is given sincerely. As for the higher figure of seven-hundred, this is not guaranteed. The extent of the degree of multiplication depends on many factors, most significantly your sincerity and the value of the item given. For example, if a very wealthy person donates a thousand dollars, it cannot equate to a destitute individual who sees a hungry child and donates his only meal to that child out of mercy, thus depriving himself of nourishment. In terms of monetary value, the destitute individual has donated significantly less than a thousand dollars. However, that one meal (valued at only a few dollars) was worth much more to the destitute individual than the thousand of the multi-millionaire, who sees that amount as pocket-change. Therefore, Allah ﷻ says, 'and Allah multiplies [the reward even more] to whoever He wills.' Thus, the multi-millionaire may well receive at least a 10x multiplication totalling the value of ten thousand, but the destitute individual may receive even more than that in return for his donated meal, if Allah ﷻ wills.

Allah ﷻ also says in the Noble Qur'an,

$$\text{لَن تَنَالُوا الْبِرَّ حَتَّىٰ تُنفِقُوا مِمَّا تُحِبُّونَ}$$

"You will never achieve righteousness until
you donate some of what you cherish." [32]

Defining the wealth that we cherish depends on who we are and how much wealth we have. The multi-millionaire does not cherish the thousand dollars in the same way that the destitute hungry person cherishes his meal. So, the destitute person donating his meal is regarded as spending from that which he loves, whilst this may not be the case for the multi-millionaire. This is how Allah judges and decides multiplied rewards based on context, which is a constant theme in the Qur'an.

In another verse, Allah ﷻ says in the Noble Qur'an,

$$\text{يَمْحَقُ اللَّهُ الرِّبَوٰا وَيُرْبِي الصَّدَقَٰتِ}$$

"Allah has made usury fruitless and charity fruitful." [33]

Allah ﷻ has made usury devoid of blessings, and has instead blessed charity and causes it to grow (يُرْبِي). The Prophet ﷺ once famously remarked,

---

[32] *Āl 'Imrān*, 92.

[33] *Al-Baqarah*, 276.

"I swear by Allah for three [qualities] which I am going to tell you about. Remember them well:

1. The wealth of a man will not diminish by charity..." [34]

There are many other verses, *ahādith*, and incidents regarding the virtue of charity.

In one famous Hadith, the Prophet  said that a man had seen a rain cloud pass by his land, causing him to hope that rain would fall upon his land. However, he heard an angel saying 'no, not here, the next land.' The man then decided to follow the path of the rain cloud, until he saw it showering rain upon his neighbour's land. Upon seeing this, he went to his neighbour and informed him of what had occurred, enquiring regarding the possible reason that the rain had fallen upon the neighbour's land and not his own. The neighbour then famously responded that from his wealth, he invests one-third back into the land for maintenance, sets aside one-third for the sustenance of his family, and donates one-third of the wealth in charity. Upon hearing this reply, the man knew that this was the reason Allah had allowed the rain cloud to burst upon the land of his neighbour and not his own.

[34] *Jāmiʿ Al-Tirmidhī.*

On the same topic, an incident from the life of 'Uthmān ibn 'Affān ﷺ is also very relevant. During the era of the caliphate of Abū Bakr al-Ṣiddīq ﷺ there was a massive drought. People were dying of starvation due to drought. Before this drought, 'Uthmān ibn 'Affān ﷺ had sent 100 camels to Syria for his own business. When the camels returned, the drought was in full force, which was completely unforeseen by 'Uthmān ibn 'Affān ﷺ. The camels had fatefully returned at a time of need, being a source of food, drink, and nourishment. The businessmen at the time approached 'Uthmān ﷺ and said that they would purchase his goods for a 20% profit above the market price. 'Uthmān ﷺ countered, and said that he had an offer for more than this amount. They continued to bargain until they reached double the price of the goods. 'Uthmān ﷺ again said he had an offer of more than this. They then asked him regarding who could possibly have offered him more than double the amount, when they were the only rich people of Madinah. 'Uthmān ﷺ then replied that Allah ﷻ has promised him that he shall receive 10 times more at a bare minimum: therefore all these camels are now freed for Allah's ﷻ sake for the people of Madinah. The generosity of 'Uthmān ibn 'Affān ﷺ became famous, as he continuously donated selflessly, such as the well of *Bi'r Rūmah* and at the expedition of Tabūk. This led our Prophet ﷺ to praise the generosity of 'Uthmān ﷺ, remarking that due to his benevolent charitableness he has been forgiven completely. Despite his selfless charitableness, 'Uthmān ﷺ remained wealthy until the end of his life, which shows us that when you give, Allah ﷻ gives back to you. You will never become poor when giving for the sake of Allah ﷻ. This is the reality in every society, where we find a group of people who are always at the forefront of donating to charities and fundraising events and never stopping to do so. This is because Allah ﷻ continues to give.

Another lesson we learn from this parable is that when we plant something, we must not just leave it be without any care. In order to see results, some effort and wisdom will be required. For example, we must choose a healthy seed to be planted in fertile soil in an area with sunlight, so that the seed will have the correct conditions and nutrients to grow. If the seed is not healthy, there is no sunlight, or the soil is inappropriate, the plant will not grow well. Similarly, charity must be given appropriately. We must search for and invest in the best forms of charity, which will ultimately give us the greatest yield and reward from Allah ﷻ. In this searching process, there are blessings too. Searching for fertile soil is similar to searching for the best forms of transitive charity, and ensuring sunlight is similar to ensuring our sincerity (*ikhlāṣ*).

Allah ﷻ concludes the verse containing the parable we have explored with the statement, 'Allah is All-Bountiful, All-Knowing.' The 'All-Bountiful' (*al-Wāsiʿ*) is a name of Allah ﷻ used eight times in the Qur'an. On seven of those occasions, the context is charity and poverty. By using this name, Allah ﷻ is telling us not to worry, for He is vast and possesses everything, He abundantly gives without end, and He will take care of us. All of this does not diminish

the power and might of Allah ﷻ in the slightest. Allah ﷻ is telling us that there is no need to worry about poverty when we have an Allah ﷻ who is All-Bountiful. On one occasion, the Prophet ﷺ saw Bilāl ؓ giving charity, despite being a freed slave and poor himself. The Prophet ﷺ said to Bilāl ؓ, 'O Bilāl! Give more charity and never fear that the Lord of the Throne will make you poor, for that will not happen. Allah ﷻ is the Lord of the Throne; He will not make you poor if you give for His sake.'

The other name of Allah ﷻ used at the conclusion of this verse is the 'All-Knowing' (al-ʿAlīm). We learn from this name of Allah ﷻ that He knows who is donating, why they are donating, and their intention for donating. Because He is 'All-Knowing', He knows who to reward and to which degree to reward; whether that be multiplied ten times, fifty times, one-hundred times, seven-hundred times, or whatever reward He wills.

In summary, whenever we intend to donate in charity, ponder upon this verse, conduct research, and make smart choices. You should choose the best soil, the best forms of charity, and diversify your investments for the sake of Allah ﷻ—for we do not know which charity will give us back 10, which will give us 50, and which will give us 700 or more. Donate to the orphans, various causes around the globe, a local *masjid*, and your family and friends that are in need. We conclude with one Hadith of the Prophet ﷺ, who was reported to have said that Allah ﷻ accepts charity with His right hand, and both of His hands are right. Allah ﷻ then nourishes that charity with the same degree of love that a person exhibits when taking care of his firstborn animal. For instance, when a person's prized steed gives birth, he or she nourishes it and take care of it, as it is a precious item. Allah will take care of this charity with more love than a person would have for his or her firstborn horse. This charity will then continue to grow, until a morsel you had donated will meet you on the Day of Judgment, having grown to the size of the mountain of Uḥud (a mountain range two kilometres long, covering one-third of Madinah). If this is the growth of one morsel, then imagine a full piece of bread! Allah ﷻ is All-Bountiful, and the more we give, the more He will multiply our charities. May Allah ﷻ make us from amongst those who donate and whose donations are accepted.

5

Safeguarding the Reward of Charity:
Pitfalls to Avoid

In verse 264 of *Sūrah al-Baqarah*, Allah ﷻ presents another parable related to donating. However, this particular parable is slightly different, for it is a parable found within an analogy. Allah ﷻ says,

يَا أَيُّهَا الَّذِينَ آمَنُوا لَا تُبْطِلُوا صَدَقَاتِكُم بِالْمَنِّ وَالْأَذَىٰ

"O believers! Do not waste your charity with reminders [of your generosity] or hurtful words." [35]

We are informed that by doing two things, all our charity will be wasted and unrewarded.

THE PARABLES OF THE QUR'AN

---

[35] *Al-Baqarah*, 264.

1. المَنُّ—'al-mann' is explicitly reminding a person of a favour you have done for them.

2. الأَذَى—'al-adhā' is any form of implicitly hurtful words or behaviour aimed at the recipients of the charity, such as sarcasm, mockery, or making them feel inferior in any way for having taken charity.

The goal of both these despicable actions is the same—reminding a needy person that you have done them a favour. Allah ﷻ informs us in the Qur'anic verse that such contemptible behaviour will eradicate your own charity, leaving you with no benefit in this world or the next. In order to emphasise the gravity of this issue and strike the hearts of the believers, Allah ﷻ continues by providing a clear example,

كَالَّذِي يُنفِقُ مَالَهُ رِئَاءَ النَّاسِ وَلَا يُؤْمِنُ بِاللَّهِ وَالْيَوْمِ الْآخِرِ

"[the one who does that is] like those who donate their wealth just to show off and do not believe in Allah or the Last Day." [36]

Upon reading this example, a true believer would look in disdain on the foolishness of such an individual who donates just to show off, without having sincerely believed. This is the way of the hypocrites, who are not recompensed by Allah ﷻ

---

[36] Ibid.

for any supposed good they do. However, what is even more astonishing is that Allah  is saying that the believer who follows his donations with *al-mann* and *al-adhā* is of a similar state! In the same way that the hypocrites are not recompensed due to their corrupt intentions, these believers will not be recompensed for their charity either, even though their original intention was sincere. This is due to the destructive power of *al-mann* and *al-adhā*.

Allah ⚚ is thus telling us not to go down that path of destruction. We must keep our intentions sincere, acknowledging that the wealth we are donating is a blessing from Allah ⚚. He is the one who granted us this wealth, and He is doing us a favour by allowing us to donate it generously. Allah ⚚ then favours us again by accepting that good donation and deed, even though that wealth originally belonged to Him. Thus, the deed is not originally ours. The moment we begin to think that we are the ones doing the good deed and giving our wealth, we have put our charity in jeopardy. We have opened the door to *al-mann* and *al-adhā*. Allah ⚚ is saying that we then might as well be like the hypocrite mentioned in the verse, as the end result of your deeds and rewards being wasted will be the same. The only difference was that the hypocrite's intention was corrupt from the start, whilst our intention transfigures after doing the deed due to committing *al-mann* and *al-adhā*.

When Ā'ishah ⚚ would donate to charity, she would rub together the gold and silver coins in order to clean them, after which she would perfume them. When questioned as to why she did that, she said, *'Do you not realise that I am giving this wealth in front of Allah!'* She had recognised the reality that it is not the beggar to whom the wealth directly goes, but it is to Allah ﷻ, Who will accept her charity after it is received. Hence, she would choose the best of wealth to be donated. This is unlike us today, who choose the worst wealth to be donated, such as the most crumpled of our currency notes.

Allah ﷻ further says,

$$\text{فَمَثَلُهُ كَمَثَلِ صَفْوَانٍ عَلَيْهِ تُرَابٌ فَأَصَابَهُ وَابِلٌ فَتَرَكَهُ صَلْدًا}$$
$$\text{لَّا يَقْدِرُونَ عَلَى شَيْءٍ مِّمَّا كَسَبُوا}$$

"Their example [the people who donate without faith or to show off] is that of a hard barren rock covered with a thin layer of soil hit by a strong rain—leaving it just a bare stone. Such people are unable to preserve the reward of their charity." [37]

The analogy here is that the heart of the one who rejects Allah ﷻ is like a hard rock. A hard rock indicates that the heart will not be soft when thinking of Allah ﷻ or the poor. When something beneficial comes upon it, the hard rock will repel it. This is the state of the heart of a hypocrite or disbeliever, in contrast to the heart of a sincere believer

---

[37] Ibid.

whose heart is like fertile soil that accepts and absorbs beneficial rain. Allah ﷻ then says that the hypocrite or disbeliever will occasionally attempt to beautify that rock by having a thin albeit false layer of good soil (deeds) upon it. He utilises these false good deeds to give an illusion. However, the blessed rain (the Qur'an) of Allah ﷻ then descends and reveals the truth. When this rain comes, it washes away the illusion and exposes the reality underneath for all to witness. Every person then recognises that this individual was not a true believer, but a hypocrite.

This analogy compares beautifully to the previous verse, wherein Allah ﷻ says that when a righteous person plants a seed, it becomes seven-hundred grains. As for the *kāfir*, he does not even have fertile soil in which to plant a seed. This is the great contrast between a believer and a hypocrite.

Allah ﷻ says regarding insincere actions in the Qur'an,

وَ قَدِمْنَآ اِلٰى مَا عَمِلُوْا مِنْ عَمَلٍ فَجَعَلْنٰهُ هَبَآءً مَّنْثُوْرًا

"All the good that they have done, we will cause it to scatter like dust." [38]

This is because insincere actions are not solid, so they easily scatter and dissipate like dust. As for that which is done sincerely for the sake of Allah, it is firm, solid, and remains.

---

[38] Ibid.

Allah ﷻ says that any good action done egotistically—such as charity followed by *al-mann* and *al-adhā*—falls under the same category as doing something insincerely for the sake of other than Allah ﷻ. Therefore, whenever we donate in charity, we should be thankful to Allah ﷻ that He has blessed us with the opportunity to give and should avoid *al-mann* and *al-adhā* at all costs.

Another important point to be noted here is that Allah ﷻ considers the feelings of the poor. No one wishes to be poor such that they have to accept charity. Thus, Allah ﷻ instructs us not to humiliate the poor or make them feel bad, for if we do so Allah ﷻ will remove our blessings.

Always remember that we should thank Allah that we are in good financial circumstances and that we are not doing a favour to those who are less fortunate by giving. Rather, Allah ﷻ is doing us a favour by granting us opportunities to donate. When we do so sincerely, we are planting seeds that will each sprout seven-hundred grains that will continuously benefit us. On the other hand, if we donate for the wrong reasons, our hearts are like covered, hard rocks that give only false illusions of being good, ready to be exposed at any time.

We ask Allah ﷻ for divine enablement and guidance.

6

Towards Investing for the Hereafter:
The Virtues of Charity

The next parable we will be discussing is found in verse 265 of *Sūrah al-Baqarah,* continuing a sequence of four parables regarding charity found in just one page of the Qur'an. This is a great mercy of Allah ﷻ, as He provides so many examples, inspirations, and parables regarding charity. This is all to ingrain in us the understanding that donating in charity sincerely is like a guaranteed profitable investment, the returns of which will certainly come back to us manifold. If we invest appropriately whilst fulfilling all the conditions, we will become affluent in this world and the Hereafter. However, if we do not invest properly, it will be an investment that crashes to zero and leaves us bankrupt.

In verse 265, Allah ﷻ says,

وَمَثَلُ الَّذِينَ يُنفِقُونَ أَمْوَالَهُمُ ابْتِغَاءَ مَرْضَاتِ اللَّهِ وَتَثْبِيتًا مِّنْ أَنفُسِهِمْ كَمَثَلِ جَنَّةٍ بِرَبْوَةٍ أَصَابَهَا وَابِلٌ فَآتَتْ أُكُلَهَا ضِعْفَيْنِ فَإِن لَّمْ يُصِبْهَا وَابِلٌ فَطَلٌّ وَاللَّهُ بِمَا تَعْمَلُونَ بَصِيرٌ

"And the example of those who donate their wealth, seeking Allah's pleasure and as a reaffirmation of their own faith, is that of a garden on a fertile hill: when heavy rain falls, it yields up twice its normal produce. If no heavy rain falls, a drizzle is sufficient. And Allah is All-Seeing of what you do." [39]

In this verse, we are given the example of a garden (*jannah*) on a moderately elevated fertile hill (*rabwah*). A beautiful point regarding the vastness of the Arabic language is that it has a specific word that describes a place of moderate elevation—*rabwah*. Why is it beneficial to have a garden at a *rabwah*? This is because at a certain moderate level of elevation, the soil, water, and climate are conducive to ensuring the growth of the best crop. This is something known to adept farmers.

Some scholars opine that this is another parable for charity being similar to an investment that gives you more than just what you put in, similar to the previous parable in

---

[39] *Al-Baqarah*, 265.

Sūrah al-Baqarah. Other scholars opine that this parable is informing us that the one who gives his wealth for the sake of Allah ﷻ and as a reaffirmation of his own faith benefits in another way. For it is as if he has a massively profitable investment and a permanent source of unexpected extra income in the form of the garden at the *rabwah*. Thus, when you give for the sake of Allah ﷻ, your wealth continually increases, and Allah ﷻ provides for you from sources you never expected or fathomed. This is a concept supported in other Qur'anic verses and *aḥādīth*.

Another interesting benefit of this verse can be derived from the condition *'and as a reaffirmation of their own faith.'* This powerful clause is in relation to the doubts that can creep into the hearts of people when donating, regarding whether they will truly receive multiplied rewards in return. This clause clarifies that the faith of the true believers reaffirms that they will still give for the sake of Allah ﷻ, thus battling and defeating their own internal doubts. It is a powerful phrase to ponder upon before donating. Other scholars opine that there is another explanation for this clause. They say that there are two types of reaffirmation (*tathbīt*): internal and external. Through internal *tathbīt* you reaffirm your own intentions, ensuring that you are acting for the sake of Allah ﷻ and overcoming your doubts. Through external *tathbīt*, you verify and research the causes you are donating to. You search for the best causes and places to donate to, and do not give wealth haphazardly. This is a praiseworthy habit we should build, as unfortunately, we do not always do our

due diligence before donating. We should aim to verify and diversify our donations, just as we verify and diversify our investments to ensure maximum profits. We should choose different types of charities; local and international, friends and family, widows and orphans, refugees, and anyone else who needs our help across the globe. We will be rewarded by Allah ﷻ for our diligence and diversification.

There are many stories of the noble Companions ﷢ and pious predecessors ﷭ exhibiting their pure intentions, and how they would determine who was most deserving of their charity. If we follow their wonderful example, Allah ﷻ says that He guarantees us a profitable investment with minimal effort. He will give us a garden situated at an ideal location; we will not need to provide water for it, because the water will rain upon it and come from the mountains. Despite minimal effort, our investment will be guaranteed to multiply.

Allah ﷻ then provides a final example regarding the one who donates without faith in Allah ﷻ. Allah ﷻ says,

أَيَوَدُّ أَحَدُكُمْ أَن تَكُونَ لَهُۥ جَنَّةٌ مِّن نَّخِيلٍ وَأَعْنَابٍ تَجْرِى مِن تَحْتِهَا ٱلْأَنْهَٰرُ لَهُۥ فِيهَا مِن كُلِّ ٱلثَّمَرَٰتِ وَأَصَابَهُ ٱلْكِبَرُ وَلَهُۥ ذُرِّيَّةٌ ضُعَفَآءُ فَأَصَابَهَآ إِعْصَارٌ فِيهِ نَارٌ فَٱحْتَرَقَتْ ۗ كَذَٰلِكَ يُبَيِّنُ ٱللَّهُ لَكُمُ ٱلْءَايَٰتِ لَعَلَّكُمْ تَتَفَكَّرُونَ

"Would any of you wish to have a garden with palm trees, grapevines, and all kinds of fruits with rivers flowing underneath and as they grow very old with dependent children, a fiery whirlwind hits the garden, burning it all up? This is how Allah makes His revelations clear to you, so perhaps you will reflect."[40]

Previously, in verse 264, the example was given of the person who donates for the sake of Allah, and the person who donates for the sake of reminding others of their generosity and to harm others (*al-mann* and *al-adhā*). In this verse, a similar example is given of a person who gives for the sake of Allah ﷻ and a person who gives without faith. This emphasises the importance of intentions, as a good deed performed with the right intention becomes a massively profitable investment, whilst the same deed performed improperly will give back zero profits.

---

[40] *Al-Baqarah*, 266.

7

Spending Sincerely
for the Sake of Allah

In verse 266 of *Sūrah al-Baqarah*, Allah ﷻ asks a rhetorical question in the final parable of this section,

أَيَوَدُّ أَحَدُكُمْ أَن تَكُونَ لَهُ جَنَّةٌ مِّن نَّخِيلٍ وَأَعْنَابٍ تَجْرِى مِن تَحْتِهَا ٱلْأَنْهَٰرُ لَهُ فِيهَا مِن كُلِّ ٱلثَّمَرَٰتِ وَأَصَابَهُ ٱلْكِبَرُ وَلَهُ ذُرِّيَّةٌ ضُعَفَآءُ فَأَصَابَهَآ إِعْصَارٌ فِيهِ نَارٌ فَٱحْتَرَقَتْ ۗ كَذَٰلِكَ يُبَيِّنُ ٱللَّهُ لَكُمُ ٱلْءَايَٰتِ لَعَلَّكُمْ تَتَفَكَّرُونَ

"Would any of you wish to have a garden with palm trees, grapevines, and all kinds of fruits with rivers flowing underneath and as they grow very old with dependent children, a fiery whirlwind hits the garden, burning it all up? This is how Allah makes His revelations clear to you, so perhaps you will reflect." [41]

THE PARABLES OF THE QURAN

---

[41] *Al-Baqarah*, 266.

Allah ﷻ is presenting the case of an individual who owns a lush garden that contains a variety of valuable fruits and plants. The owner is profiting and benefitting from this garden, without having to lift a finger. This owner then becomes elderly and has young children, such that he becomes preoccupied and unable to undertake strenuous activity due to his age. Eventually, the time comes for this owner to leave this world and die. At this point, he needs to leave this ideal garden as a legacy for his young children, for they are still dependant, unable to earn for themselves, and do not have another source of income. However, in this sensitive situation, a ravaging fire-filled tornado razes and devastates the garden.

In this parable, Allah ﷻ is telling us that the person who donates wealth for the sake of showing off is similar to the person who owns a lush garden. However, when he is most in need of this lush garden on the Day of Judgement for harvesting rewards (similar to how the elderly owner needs it when passing away for the sake of his dependent children), it is completely obliterated before his eyes and absolutely nothing is left salvageable. Allah ﷻ is posing a rhetorical question in this verse, asking us if we would wish to be that unfortunate man. We would obviously not, for this unfortunate individual was deceived. This is because he did not act and donate for the sake of Allah ﷻ. Such an insincere donator would think that he has dazzled by donating thousands of dollars, so he would be deserving of a prime reward. However, as he donated to impress people and not for the sake of Allah ﷻ, on the Day of Judgement his situation will be as Allah ﷻ vividly describes,

وَقَدِمْنَا إِلَىٰ مَا عَمِلُوا مِنْ عَمَلٍ فَجَعَلْنَاهُ هَبَاءً مَّنثُورًا

"Then We will turn to whatever [good] deeds they did,
reducing them to scattered dust." [42]

This parable makes us understand that if we perform a good
deed with an impure intention, the deed might appear good to
people, but it will in reality be of no benefit or value for us in
the Hereafter. More broadly, if any action is not done purely
for Allah's ﷻ sake, then that action is of no value. Thus, the
garden of the one who gives for the sake of Allah will last
many generations, as mentioned earlier in *Sūrah al-Baqarah.*
But the garden of the one who gives for the sake of his own
ego will be completely obliterated when he most needs it.

In the next verse, Allah ﷻ mentions,

الشَّيْطَانُ يَعِدُكُمُ الْفَقْرَ وَيَأْمُرُكُم بِالْفَحْشَاءِ ۖ وَاللَّهُ يَعِدُكُم مَّغْفِرَةً مِّنْهُ وَفَضْلًا

"The Devil threatens you with [the prospect of] poverty
and bids you to the shameful deed [of stinginess], while
Allah promises you forgiveness and [great] bounties from
Him. And Allah is All-Bountiful, All-Knowing." [43]

THE PARABLES OF THE QURAN

---

[42] *Al-Furqān*, 23.

[43] *Al-Baqarah*, 268.

This means that the Devil will come and whisper to you that you should not donate, positing that you require the wealth for yourself and your family, and that if you do donate it will make you poor. However, in contrast, Allah ﷻ promises forgiveness and mercy—the things we are desperately in need of. This is in addition to the multiplied rewards Allah ﷻ will certainly grant, which have been mentioned later to show that forgiveness and mercy are even more important than our investment returns.

Therefore, we see that there is a conflict between the promise of the *Shayṭān* and the promise of Allah ﷻ. The *Shayṭān* is telling you to be stingy and not donate, as it will make you poor. Allah ﷻ is telling you to donate and that you shall be forgiven and given more. Which promise are we going to believe?

May we all be given the divine enablement to donate for the sake of Allah ﷻ. Knowledge is useless if it is not acted upon, so may Allah ﷻ make us amongst those who understand knowledge and act upon it.

8

A Vivid Warning Against Those Who Consume and Benefit from Interest

Beginning from the Verse of the Throne, the concluding portion of *Sūrah al-Baqarah* focusses mainly on charity and wealth. In the very last section of the chapter, on multiple occasions, Allah ﷻ also discusses and contrasts charity with its opposite concept, namely interest (*ribā*). In verse 275, Allah ﷻ provides a unique parable about interest in order to show the gravity of it. Allah ﷻ says,

الَّذِينَ يَأْكُلُونَ الرِّبَا لَا يَقُومُونَ إِلَّا كَمَا يَقُومُ الَّذِي يَتَخَبَّطُهُ الشَّيْطَانُ مِنَ الْمَسِّ

"Those who consume interest will stand [on Judgment Day] like those driven to madness by Satan's touch." [44]

---

[44] *Al-Baqarah*, 275.

This parable uses particularly a powerful language, as no person physically consumes the wealth of interest. Rather, through such a statement Allah ﷻ is drawing our attention to the negative effects of dealing with interest wealth. The food and clothes that have been purchased with such wealth are devoid of blessings, and it is as if that forbidden wealth has become part of your flesh. It is as if the food and clothing purchased with such wealth is now within and upon your body.

If we scrutinise the verse in further detail, we find that Allah ﷻ uses the verb,

$$يَتَخَبَّطُ$$

This verb has been loosely translated above as 'stand'. However, it can be more comprehensively defined as a manner of crooked walking, in which a person deviates, acts strangely, and flails his limbs in a way that leaves him prone to tumbling. Further on in the verse, the word,

$$الْمَسِّ$$

refers to madness or insanity. Allah ﷻ is saying that on the Day of Judgement, the consumer of interest wealth will be walking like a disorientated person who has been driven insane by the Devil.

According to the scholars, the intended metaphor here is that on the Day of Resurrection the people who consumed interest will be made to rise from their graves in a frightening and undignified manner, as if they have lost all their senses. On that day, all of them will be identified as the ones who dealt with interest; they will be recognised by their lack of control over their limbs, as they continuously stumble and struggle to move.

The great scholar Ibn ʿĀshūr also comments that in addition to warning those who consume interest, this verse is primarily a threat to those who justify consuming it. This point is understood from the next part of the verse,

ذَٰلِكَ بِأَنَّهُمْ قَالُوا إِنَّمَا الْبَيْعُ مِثْلُ الرِّبَا، وَأَحَلَّ اللَّهُ الْبَيْعَ وَحَرَّمَ الرِّبَا

"That [standing on Judgment Day like those driven to madness by Satan's touch] is because they say, 'Trade is no different than interest.' But Allah has permitted trading and forbidden interest." [45]

Thus, the stern punishment mentioned in this verse has been reserved for the flagrant sinner who openly challenges the Shariah of Allah ﷻ and justifies the sin without any regret or remorse. Committing the sin is blameworthy in itself but justifying it is a form of disbelief (*kufr*). As a matter of distinction, a sinner who acknowledges his sin has the hope of being forgiven, as he has an inner realisation of his misdeeds, which may lead him to regret and repentance. On the other

THE PARABLES OF THE QUR'AN

---
[45] Ibid.

hand, the sinner who justifies a sin and challenges Allah's law by putting his own opinions above his Creator's will has fallen into a deep pit of rejection that is difficult to escape from. Seldom will such an arrogant individual realise his error and be blessed to repent. This is why the verse primarily addresses such individuals so sternly, warning mankind from being from amongst these wretched souls.

Some scholars present another interpretation of the metaphor found in the verse, postulating that Allah ﷻ is describing the sorry state of the interest-consumers in this world and not in the Hereafter. Allah ﷻ is saying that such people who deal in interest may be seen as dignified or respectable in society, but in reality, their hearts and souls are in turmoil. They publicly feign happiness but are full of inner emptiness, without understanding its reason. They are aimlessly wandering in their private lives due to metaphorical insanity. This is all because they preposterously claim that common trade is the same as interest, blatantly ignoring that Allah ﷻ has made one lawful whilst rendering the other unlawful.

From amongst the various ways of dealing in interest, the most severe is giving a loan whilst charging interest, under the pretext that it is similar to a trade deal. This is not the same as being in a position where you are forced to give interest. For example, they say that buying a cloth for $10 and selling it for $15 with a $5 profit is exactly the same as loaning out $10 and taking back $15 with a similar profit. However, Allah ﷻ says that buying and selling merchandise is not comparable to buying and selling currency in the form of a loan, as people usually only take loans due to dire and desperate situations, which is not the case for purchasing general merchandise. Thus, due to desperate circumstances, a person may be compelled to take a usurious loan that he or she may struggle to repay. Many lenders will then use this as an opportunity to exploit such financially desperate individuals with extortionate and ever-rising interest rates. This is in contrast to the Islamic spirit that encourages us to give goodly loans (*qarḍ ḥasan*) for the sake of Allah  and anticipating reward.

From a historical perspective, we should also be aware that the concept of interest was banned for most of European history. In fact, it only became legal in Europe around four-hundred years ago. Prior to this there were multiple death penalties in place for those who charged interest. In fact, in medieval times, a particular King of England banned people of the Jewish faith from the country because he felt they were giving usurious loans to others, and these loans were destroying society. We learn from this that the interest-fuelled economy that unfortunately exists today is a recent development.

To conclude, in verse 279, Allah ﷻ addresses those who justify taking interest by informing them that if they do not give up outstanding interest, then,

فَأْذَنُوا بِحَرْبٍ مِّنَ اللَّهِ وَرَسُولِهِ

"Beware of a war with Allah and His Messenger!" [46]

In this verse, Allah ﷻ warns us that if we charge interest, it is as if we are possessed by the *Shayṭān*, and that we are declaring war on Allah ﷻ and his Messenger ﷺ. This verse has also been used to prove that dealing in the dark arts (*siḥr*) and jinn possession (*mass*) are realities, since Allah is describing the one who takes interest is as someone who is possessed.

---

[46] *Al-Baqarah*, 279.

9

Holding Tightly and
Firmly to the
Divine Rope of Allah

In verse 102 of *Sūrah Āl 'Imrān*, Allah ﷻ sets up the very first parable of the chapter by saying,

يَٰٓأَيُّهَا الَّذِينَ ءَامَنُوا اتَّقُوا اللهَ حَقَّ تُقَٰتِهِ وَلَا تَمُوتُنَّ إِلَّا وَأَنتُم مُّسْلِمُونَ

"O believers! Be mindful of Allah in the way He deserves, and do not die except in [a state of full] submission [to Him]." [47]

In the following verse, Allah ﷻ then begins the actual parable,

وَاعْتَصِمُوا بِحَبْلِ اللهِ جَمِيعًا وَلَا تَفَرَّقُوا وَاذْكُرُوا نِعْمَتَ اللهِ عَلَيْكُمْ إِذْ كُنتُمْ أَعْدَآءً فَأَلَّفَ بَيْنَ قُلُوبِكُمْ فَأَصْبَحْتُم بِنِعْمَتِهِ إِخْوَٰنًا وَكُنتُمْ عَلَىٰ شَفَا حُفْرَةٍ مِّنَ النَّارِ فَأَنقَذَكُم مِّنْهَاۗ كَذَٰلِكَ يُبَيِّنُ اللهُ لَكُمْ ءَايَٰتِهِ لَعَلَّكُمْ تَهْتَدُونَ

---

47 *Āl 'Imrān*, 102.

"And hold firmly to the rope of Allah and do not be divided. Remember Allah's favour upon you when you were enemies, then He united your hearts, so you—by His grace—became brothers. And you were at the brink of a large pit of fire and He saved you from it. This is how Allah makes His revelations clear to you, so that you may be [rightly] guided." [48]

This verse contains two instances of symbolism within it.

The first is found in,

وَاعْتَصِمُوا بِحَبْلِ اللَّهِ جَمِيعًا

"And hold firmly to the rope of Allah"

To a person precariously hanging from a cliff or a drowning person, a rope coming from above signifies that there is an overarching authority that can save you. For all of us who are precariously hanging and drowning in this world, our authority above is Allah ﷻ, who says that He has extended His rope for us. Scholars have slightly differed about the meaning of the rope of Allah ﷻ. Some posit that it is the religion of Islam, some say it is the Qur'an, whilst others postulate that it is the united Muslim nation. The most precise opinion is that the rope of Allah ﷻ is the Qur'an itself, which is supported by the Hadith in which the Prophet ﷺ said,

---

48 *Āl 'Imrān*, 103.

فَإِنَّ هَذَا الْقُرْآنَ سَبَبٌ طَرَفُهُ بِيَدِ اللهِ وَطَرَفُهُ بِأَيْدِيكُمْ فَتَمَسَّكُوا بِهِ

*"Indeed this Quran [is the rope of Allah], one end of it
is in the Hands of Allah and the other end is in
your hands, so hold onto it."* [49]

Another benefit of a rope is that it is something that is used
to pull yourself up and ascend. Similarly, the Qur'an is like a
rope that can lift you up. The Prophet ﷺ precisely said,

*"By the Qur'an, He [Allah] raises people up
and causes others to go down."*

A rope is also used to gather and tie objects. When Allah ﷻ
commands us to gather together and unite upon His rope,
He is stressing the importance of uniting on the correct
things. We should avoid uniting on our whims and desires,
but we should make our central gathering point the rope of
Allah ﷻ—the Qur'an. When we all unite upon this central
rope of salvation and cling firmly onto it, we will attain
safety. On the contrary, if we do not take hold of this rope
of salvation whilst we are precariously hanging off the tall
cliffs and drowning in the deep oceans of this world, we will
meet destruction. Choosing to let go of the rope of Allah ﷻ
is choosing to forfeit safety and hope.

70

[49] Muʿjam Al-Ṭabarānī.

The next part of the verse is regarding the Muslim community at the time. In the pre-Islamic period of ignorance (*jāhiliyyah*), due to tribal tensions, it was not even possible to imagine that the Emigrants (*Muhājirūn*) and Helpers (*Anṣār*) could become brethren. Even the Helpers had strong enmity between them, epitomised by the strife and consequent fifty-year long civil war that existed between the Aws and the Khazraj. For an entire generation they were at each other's necks. However, when they were honoured with Islam, everything changed. Allah ﷻ united the hearts of the fiercest of enemies through the bonds of faith, turning foes into brothers. In this verse, Allah ﷻ reminds the people to remember this great blessing of His upon them. In another verse, Allah ﷻ says,

وَأَلَّفَ بَيْنَ قُلُوبِهِمْ ۚ لَوْ أَنفَقْتَ مَا فِي الْأَرْضِ جَمِيعًا مَّا أَلَّفْتَ بَيْنَ قُلُوبِهِمْ وَلَٰكِنَّ اللَّهَ أَلَّفَ بَيْنَهُمْ

"He brought their hearts together. Had you spent all the riches in the earth, you could not have united their hearts. But Allah has united them." [50]

50 *Al-Anfāl*, 63.

Continuing with *Sūrah Āl 'Imrān* verse 103, the next part is where we find the second symbolic metaphor,

$$وَكُنتُمۡ عَلَىٰ شَفَا حُفۡرَةٍ مِّنَ ٱلنَّارِ فَأَنقَذَكُم مِّنۡهَا$$

"And you were at the brink of a large pit of fire and He saved you from it." [51]

A '*ḥufrah*' is a large pit. The large pit of fire mentioned in this verse symbolises the actual destructive Hellfire. Allah is saying that before embracing Islam, you were looking down whilst tethering on the edge of this pit of fire. However, when Allah honoured and blessed you with Islam, He saved you from this dangerous edge. Reiterating this message and metaphor in a Hadith, the Prophet said,

"My example with regard to you all is that of a man who is holding onto the belt of somebody who wishes to rush into the fire, telling him to come back [to safety]."

In conclusion, both of the symbolic metaphors found in verse 103 of *Sūrah Āl 'Imrān* are of outstanding beauty and eloquence. They remind us of Allah's wonderful blessings upon us, and most importantly draw our attention to the indisputable fact that the Noble Qur'an is the rope of Allah that we all need to gather upon and

---

[51] *Āl 'Imrān*, 103.

cling firmly onto as a united *ummah*. If we ever stray from the Qur'an, we will lose our way and find ourselves on the edge of a fiery pit of destruction.

May Allah ﷻ unite us upon His rope.

10

Spiritual Dimensions of
Life and Death

The next parable we will be exploring is found in verse 122 of *Sūrah al-Anʿām*, which contains a very beautiful story. To understand the context of this parable, we must first mention the infamous historical episode where the great enemy of Islam, Abū Jahl, observed the Prophet ﷺ offering prayer on one occasion. He commanded that the entrails of an animal be thrown on him whilst the crooked Meccans watched on and laughed. A relative of the Prophet ﷺ who was not yet Muslim and followed the religion of the Quraysh, Ḥamzah ؓ, was informed upon returning from an expedition as to what had occurred with the Prophet ﷺ. Ḥamzah ؓ was of a similar age to the Prophet ﷺ and was both his uncle and foster-brother, as one of the slave girls of Abū Lahab named Thuwaybah had fostered them both when they were young. Thus, Ḥamzah ؓ was enraged upon learning the whole story in regard to Abū Jahl and the Banū Makhzūm's taunting and despicable treatment of his dear relative. What worsened the matter was that the Meccans watched on and laughed without coming to his defence. This boiling rage was not based on Islam, but out of tribal pride. No other man had the courage to challenge Abū Jahl due to his status as the most-respected figure of the Banū Makhzūm. However, Ḥamzah ﷺ had the bravery to do so, as he was his equal from the Banū Hāshim. Before even returning home, Ḥamzah ﷺ took up his bow and marched right up to Abū Jahl in front of the Kaʿbah, and rebuked the wretched man as to how he had the audacity to insult his nephew in public. He then struck Abū Jahl on the face with his weapon, leaving the wretched man helpless before the anger and raw strength of the well-respected leader of the Banū Hāshim. When Abū Jahl saw the anger in Ḥamzah's ﷺ eyes, he could do nothing but cower and plea to him that the Prophet ﷺ was badmouthing the idols, considering them foolish, and making fun of their religion. Ḥamzah ﷺ then replied, "What is there not to make fun of, for you are worshipping stones that you make with your own hands!" He then recited the testimony of faith (*shahādah*). We learn from this that it was tribalism-based anger that originally caused him to proclaim the testimony of faith. He then made the historic decision to go to Dār al-Arqam and officially embrace Islam.

After this incident, as mentioned by Ibn ʿAbbās ﷺ (the nephew of Ḥamzah ﷺ), Allah ﷻ revealed the following verse regarding Ḥamzah's ﷺ reversion story,

$$\text{أَوَمَن كَانَ مَيْتًا فَأَحْيَيْنَاهُ وَجَعَلْنَا لَهُ نُورًا يَمْشِي بِهِ فِي النَّاسِ}$$
$$\text{كَمَن مَّثَلُهُ فِي الظُّلُمَاتِ لَيْسَ بِخَارِجٍ مِّنْهَا}$$

"Is it [conceivable] that the one who was dead and to whom We gave life, and set for him a light with which he walks among men, [is held to] be like the one whose condition is such that he is in total darkness, never coming out of it?" [52]

The 'One who was dead and to whom we gave life' refers to Ḥamzah ☙, who has been symbolically called 'dead' when he was previously devoid of faith. This is as a person without faith is metaphorically dead, as true life is found in Islam and the Qur'an. Allah ☙ says,

$$\text{وَكَذَلِكَ أَوْحَيْنَا إِلَيْكَ رُوحًا مِنْ أَمْرِنَا}$$

"So We have revealed a spirit to you [O Prophet] by Our command." [53]

Having a spirit (*rūḥ*) is the difference between a lifeless corpse and a living human body. Allah ☙ calls the Qur'an a 'spirit', for without the Qur'an and its perfect teachings a person is spiritually dead and lifeless. Allah ☙ also says,

[52] *Al-Anʿām*, 122.

[53] *Al-Shūrā*, 52.

$$\text{إِنْ هُمْ إِلَّا كَالْأَنْعَامِ}$$

"They are like cattle [due to not having faith]"

In many other instances in the Qur'an, Allah ﷻ likens disbelief to death and faith to life. For example, Allah ﷻ says,

$$\text{يَا أَيُّهَا الَّذِينَ آمَنُوا اسْتَجِيبُوا لِلَّهِ وَلِلرَّسُولِ إِذَا دَعَاكُمْ لِمَا يُحْيِيكُمْ}$$

"O believers! Respond to Allah and His Messenger when he calls you to that which gives you life." [54]

If we do not respond to that which will give us true life, then we may as well be dead.

Similarly, Ḥamzah ﷺ was spiritually dead and was brought back to life through the blessings of faith. He was given a light to walk in,

$$\text{وَجَعَلْنَا لَهُ نُورًا يَمْشِي بِهِ فِي النَّاسِ}$$

"And We set for him a light with which he walks among men." [55]

---

[54] *Al-Anfāl*, 24.

[55] *Al-Anʿām*, 122.

The Qur'an is the epitome of such light,

$$وَأَنزَلْنَا إِلَيْكُمْ نُورًا مُّبِينًا$$

"And We have sent down to you a brilliant light." [56]

Another powerful Qur'anic metaphor is its presentation of light representing guidance and darkness representing misguidance. Allah ﷻ says,

$$يُخْرِجُهُم مِّنَ الظُّلُمَاتِ إِلَى النُّورِ$$

"He brings them out of darkness [misguidance] and into light [guidance]." [57]

Light enables a person to clearly observe their surroundings, situate themselves, and see the path to their destination, thus giving purpose and meaning to life. Without light a person will be lost, stuck, and unable to reach his or her destination even if it is known, thus having no real purpose and meaning in life.

THE PARABLES OF THE QURAN

[56] *Al-Nisā'*, 174.

[57] *Al-Baqarah*, 257.

That is why Allah says,

$$\text{كَمَن مَّثَلُهُ فِي الظُّلُمَاتِ لَيْسَ بِخَارِجٍ مِّنْهَا}$$

"[Can the one previously dead who was given life and a guiding light] be like the one whose condition is such that he is in total darkness, never coming out of it?"

In this part of the verse, 'the one whose condition is such that he is in total darkness' originally refers to Abū Jahl, but this description can also be extended similarly to every purposeless disbeliever who wanders aimlessly and sees no higher cause. As for the one who was given life and a guiding light, this originally refers to Ḥamzah ﷺ. This description can also extend to any God-conscious and faithful believer who adheres to the teachings of the Noble Qur'an.

What a beautiful story and parable we find in this marvellous verse of the Qur'an!

11

The Panting Dog:
A Warning Against the Immoral and Corrupt Scholar

Verses 175 and 176 of *Sūrah al-ʿArāf* recount an incident from the Children of Israel. Recounting such peculiar yet meaningful incidents of the Children of Israel has many benefits, which is why the Prophet ﷺ encouraged the telling of such accounts. The Qur'anic verses presenting this particular incident also contain a parable that sends shivers down our spines. In fact, these terrifying verses contain arguably the harshest descriptive similitude of the Qur'an; such a similitude which the scholars mention in their speech and writings with a clear sense of fear and trepidation.

Allah ﷺ says,

وَاتْلُ عَلَيْهِمْ نَبَأَ الَّذِي آتَيْنَاهُ آيَاتِنَا فَانْسَلَخَ مِنْهَا فَأَتْبَعَهُ الشَّيْطَانُ فَكَانَ مِنَ الْغَاوِينَ. وَلَوْ شِئْنَا لَرَفَعْنَاهُ بِهَا وَلَكِنَّهُ أَخْلَدَ إِلَى الْأَرْضِ وَاتَّبَعَ هَوَاهُ فَمَثَلُهُ كَمَثَلِ الْكَلْبِ إِنْ تَحْمِلْ عَلَيْهِ يَلْهَثْ أَوْ تَتْرُكْهُ يَلْهَثْ ذَلِكَ مَثَلُ الْقَوْمِ الَّذِينَ كَذَّبُوا بِآيَاتِنَا

"And relate to them [O Prophet] the story of the one to whom We gave Our signs, but he abandoned them, so Satan took hold of him, and he became a deviant. If We had willed, We would have elevated him with Our signs, but he clung to this life—following his evil desires. His example is that of a dog: if you chase it away, it pants, and if you leave it, it [still] pants. This is the example of the people who deny Our signs. So narrate [to them] stories [of the past], so perhaps they will reflect." [58]

The Qur'anic exegetes inform us that these verses present the sad story of a man from the Children of Israel named Balʿam ibn Bāʿūrāʾ. He was an adept scholar and worshipper who lived at the time of Mūsā ﷺ, but later deviated from the truth.

The verses begin with an instruction to the Prophet ﷺ, 'And relate to them [O Prophet] the story of the one to whom We gave Our signs'. The sign being referred to here is the divinely inspired memorisation and knowledge of the Torah given to Balʿam ibn Bāʿūrāʾ. Despite being blessed with divine knowledge and other special talents, Allah ﷺ

---

[58] *Al-ʿArāf*, 175-176.

describes Balʿam's subsequent behaviour with the verb *'fansalakha'*, which literally translates as 'to peel off'. This is because Balʿam abandoned and did not act upon his knowledge, causing it to loosely peel off him and not remain as a source of benefit. Allah ﷻ then informs us that Balʿam had the potential to reach the highest stations of nobility by virtue of knowledge, which is a blessing that Allah bestows on selected servants of His as a means of elevating their ranks,

يَرْفَعِ اللَّهُ الَّذِينَ آمَنُوا مِنكُمْ وَالَّذِينَ أُوتُوا الْعِلْمَ دَرَجَاتٍ

"Allah will elevate those of you who are faithful, and [raise] those gifted with knowledge in rank." [59]

Shockingly, despite the great status of the religious knowledge he possessed, Balʿam was condemned due to pursuing evil desires, acting oblivious towards the demands of his knowledge, and maintaining a desire to live permanently on this earth. He made a foolish trade of the heights of eternal Paradise in exchange for the lowliness of this temporary world.

Due to his extreme foolhardiness, Allah ﷻ stated that 'his example is that of a dog: if you chase it away it pants, and if you leave it, it [still] pants'. This description demonstrates the wild nature of such a dog. It does not understand commands of any sort and is continuously panting at all times, oblivious of who it was before.

---

[59] *Al-Mujādilah*, 11.

The scholars have presented varying stories as to how Bal'am ended up in such a damning predicament. Some opine that he was continuously tempted and seduced by a pagan king to join him in opposing Mūsā ﷺ. He initially refused, but after multiple attempts the pagan king was able to corrupt him and bribe him with lavish promises of fame, power, wealth, and women. Once Bal'am had received a taste of these worldly luxuries and pleasures, he became intoxicated by them and began using his divinely bestowed knowledge for evil purposes. He began utilising his scholarship and talents for falsehood in order to harm the Children of Israel, until a time came where Mūsā ﷺ overcame him and put an end to his mischievous delinquency and criminality.

It is due to the severity of these crimes that Allah ﷻ described him as a wild panting dog. This is a particularly powerful metaphor as Allah ﷻ did not compare him to admired creatures from the marvellous animal kingdom, such as the brave lion or the sharp falcon. Rather, Allah ﷻ deliberately chose a generally demeaned animal to compare him to; an animal that people use to insult one another universally. It is a general human convention to use the term 'dog' in a derogatory manner, but this is not to say that all dogs are considered evil. Allah ﷻ explicitly mentions in the Qur'an that you may eat from the quarry of your trained dog. As a side point, this fact again demonstrates to us the virtue of knowledge, since an untrained dog has its rank 'raised' due to its training, as if the knowledge of how to hunt has in itself given a privilege to this animal.

Among the various lessons we can take from this story and verse, the strongest lesson is for the people of knowledge, scholars, and preachers. They should constantly seek for Allah's ﷻ protection from using their knowledge to service evil. This is one the most devastating trials that can befall the Muslim *ummah*, as 'Umar Ibn al-Khaṭṭāb ؓ said,

"Islam will be demolished by the faults of [evil] scholars, the arguments of hypocrites over the Book, and the judgment of misguided leaders."

The Prophet ﷺ is reported to have said,

"There is something I fear for my Ummah more than the Dajjal...Misguided and astray scholars."

We seek Allah's ﷻ refuge from this! Unfortunately, there are many erudite scholars that have abundant knowledge. However, they falter and fail once they attain political influence and power by association with leaders and governments. The seductive power of status, wealth, and titles such as '*Shaykh*', '*Mufti*', or '*Grand Mufti*' proves too much for them to handle. Shockingly, these same scholars then go on to publicly justify oppression and evil, in some situations even cheapening the blood of the Muslims. Horrendous statements such as, 'If there are protestors in the *masjid*, go ahead and kill them', are all too common. In some situations, these scholars brazenly praise non-Muslim leaders by unbefittingly comparing them to our great and noble

predecessors, such as Khālid ibn al-Walīd ﷺ. These are the 'scholars of the rulers' (*'ulamā' al-salāṭīn*)—scholars who have sold themselves to the highest bidder. Warning against this, our Prophet ﷺ apprised the scholars regarding the harms of associating themselves with dictators and rulers. For scholarship to remain sincere and impartial it must be independent of rulers and politicians who seek to exploit the position of scholarship for their own personal gains. The scholars should be the guards against corruption and those who keep the rulers from straying, not puppets of the dictators and tyrants. The Prophet ﷺ said,

> *"I caution you from [going to] the gates of the rulers, for surely it heralds severe downfall."*

It is this exact thing that led to the downfall of the great scholar Bal'am ibn Bā'ūrā'. Unfortunately, we have plenty more Bal'ams in our time. We seek Allah's ﷻ refuge.

Although this parable describes those scholars who made a complete U-turn and sold their religion in exchange for the world, it can apply in a broader sense as well. If any one of us—who has been blessed with an amount of knowledge—abandons and does not practice whatever knowledge we have and instead follows our worldly desires, we should fear that a fraction of the example presented in the parable will apply to us. This understanding should shake us and ignite a desire within us to implement our knowledge to the best of our abilities. Such a person who has knowledge but acts as if he has none is no different to the wild panting dog that acts the same way, no matter who it was before.

Let us thank Allah ﷻ for whatever knowledge He blesses us with, and try our best to act upon it. If we ever do slip and commit a sin, let us be repentant sinners by staying far from justifying sins or knowingly misrepresenting the religion for the highest bidder.

12

The Transient and Fleeting
Nature of the World

Whenever natural or man-made disasters occur, we are accustomed to seeing images of the scenes from before and after such disasters take place. For example, we see older images of the green and luscious Amazon rainforest in comparison to recent images after deforestation and mass wildfires have ravaged the landscape. Similarly, massive wildfires have recently been decimating large areas of forestry in California, leaving beautiful landscapes blackened and charred. The reason why we are shown such images before and after the disasters by the media is to alert us to the seriousness of the issue and make us reflect. Considering this powerful effect, Allah ﷻ also uses a similar technique within various Qur'anic parables in order to alert us to certain critical realities and deliver important messages in an impactful manner.

In this chapter we will be exploring two such parables that contain similar imagery. In verse 24 of *Sūrah Yūnus*, Allah ﷻ says,

إِنَّمَا مَثَلُ الْحَيَاةِ الدُّنْيَا كَمَاءٍ أَنْزَلْنَاهُ مِنَ السَّمَاءِ فَاخْتَلَطَ بِهِ نَبَاتُ الْأَرْضِ مِمَّا يَأْكُلُ النَّاسُ وَالْأَنْعَامُ حَتَّى إِذَا أَخَذَتِ الْأَرْضُ زُخْرُفَهَا وَازَّيَّنَتْ وَظَنَّ أَهْلُهَا أَنَّهُمْ قَادِرُونَ عَلَيْهَا أَتَاهَا أَمْرُنَا لَيْلًا أَوْ نَهَارًا فَجَعَلْنَاهَا حَصِيدًا كَأَنْ لَمْ تَغْنَ بِالْأَمْسِ.

"The life of this world is just like rain We send down from the sky, producing a mixture of plants which humans and animals consume. Then just as the earth looks its best, perfectly beautified, and its people think they have full control over it, there comes to it Our command by night or by day, so We mow it down as if it never flourished yesterday!" [60]

Thereafter, in verse 45 of *Sūrah al-Kahf* a similar parable is presented,

وَاضْرِبْ لَهُمْ مَثَلَ الْحَيَاةِ الدُّنْيَا كَمَاءٍ أَنْزَلْنَاهُ مِنَ السَّمَاءِ فَاخْتَلَطَ بِهِ نَبَاتُ الْأَرْضِ فَأَصْبَحَ هَشِيمًا تَذْرُوهُ الرِّيَاحُ ۗ وَكَانَ اللَّهُ عَلَى كُلِّ شَيْءٍ مُقْتَدِرًا

"And give them a parable of this worldly life. [It is] like the plants of the earth, thriving when sustained by the rain We send down from the sky. Then they [soon] turn into chaff scattered by the wind. And Allah is fully capable of [doing] all things." [61]

---

[60] *Yūnus*, 24.

[61] *Al-Kahf*, 45.

In both these parables, Allah  compares the life of this world with land that is irrigated by rainwater from the heavens. The rainwater soaks into the soil, allows the seeds to germinate, promotes the growth of wonderfully varied vegetation that dazzles the eye, and eventually results in the generation of beautiful and delightful natural landscape. However, after having us picture such a pleasing panorama, Allah makes us picture these landscapes being utterly wrecked and reduced to nothingness either by His command (as is in *Sūrah Yūnus*) or by natural causes (as is in *Sūrah al-Kahf*).

The comparison being drawn is between this landscape and the life of man. Allah compares the origin of life with water falling from the skies—a comparison made even more interesting by the fact that we scientifically know that all living beings' lives began with water. Secondly, the mixing of this water with soil signifies the mixing of all human beings when they are formed. Thirdly, the blooming of varied vegetation signifies the differentiation in human growth, as no two humans are exactly the same. From the fruits and vegetables that grow, certain variations are eaten by humans and others are only eaten by animals. This indirectly refers to the existence of degrees of nobility and ignobility amongst beings, as some humans attain lofty degrees of nobility whilst others behave like wild animals. Such a behaviour is the result of a misplaced sense of arrogance in some people; many become deceived by the beauty and abilities they have been given. Their perceived ownership of wealth, status, possessions, and families makes them mistakenly feel a sense of eternity. Whilst frolicking in this heedless state, an unforeseen act of God suddenly strikes them and their possessions, leaving them in utter ruin. This could be anything ranging from sudden death, a divine punishment, a communal disaster, or even a crippling disease such as COVID-19. Allah ﷻ says that this could happen during the 'morning or evening', as nobody can predict the time when death and calamities will come. This is all in the divine knowledge of Allah ﷻ, for when He decrees that the Angel of Death come to a person, there is no force or power to prevent this. The soul will certainly be extracted, and that arrogant individual instantaneously goes from controlling so much to having absolutely nothing upon death. All the lush luxuries he previously possessed are mowed down as if they never flourished, turning into chaff and being scattered into non-existence by the wind.

If we today reflect on our own ancestors and the possessions they must have owned, we will be left wondering where it has all gone. Where are the buildings and homes that they developed and built? Where are the wonderful families that they reared, loved, and played with? Where are all the possessions that they owned? Where is all of that now? All of it is non-existent or in the hands of others, and we have no control over it.

فَأَصْبَحَ هَشِيمًا تَذْرُوهُ الرِّيَاحُ

"Then they [soon] turn into chaff scattered by the wind."

We must learn from the cycle of history that when we die, we will also become part of this scattered chaff. Our lives and possessions may currently seem grand and glorious, but eventually we will leave this world with nothing, just as those before us did. Even the greatest civilisations were forced to leave behind their grandest buildings such as the pyramids to others, as they themselves faded into nothingness.

$$كَأَن لَّمْ تَغْنَ بِالْأَمْسِ$$

"As if it never flourished [existed] yesterday."

The parable of *Sūrah Yūnus* is followed up by another beautiful verse,

$$وَاللَّهُ يَدْعُوا إِلَىٰ دَارِ السَّلَامِ$$

"And Allah invites [all] to the Home of Peace." [62]

For those that avoid delusion and succeed in this world, the Home of Peace (*dār al-salām*) is the ultimate abode that Allah ﷻ invites to.

Allah ﷻ also follows up the parable found in *Sūrah al-Kahf* with another beautiful reminder,

---

[62] *Yūnus*, 26.

$$\text{الْمَالُ وَالْبَنُونَ زِينَةُ الْحَيَاةِ الدُّنْيَا ۖ وَالْبَاقِيَاتُ الصَّالِحَاتُ}$$
$$\text{خَيْرٌ عِندَ رَبِّكَ ثَوَابًا وَخَيْرٌ أَمَلًا}$$

"Wealth and children are the adornment of this worldly life, but the everlasting good deeds are far better with your Lord in reward and in hope." [63]

An interesting linguistic peculiarity of this verse is that when describing good deeds, Allah ﷻ mentions the adjective before the noun, stating *al-bāqiyāt al-ṣāliḥāt* (everlasting good deeds) instead of *al-ṣāliḥāt al-bāqiyāt* (good deeds that are everlasting). This emphasises the eternal nature of good deeds.

In summary, all of these verses emphasise that the life of this world is beautiful and alluring, yet at the same time transient and deceiving. Upon reflection, we must make an earnest intention not to be deluded and deceived by this world.

$$\text{كُلُّ نَفْسٍ ذَآئِقَةُ الْمَوْتِ}$$

"Every soul will taste death." [64]

We may enjoy this world within the limits Allah ﷻ has set, but we should always remember that our ultimate reality is the next life. May Allah ﷻ make us amongst those who are successful in the next life.

---

[63] *Al-Kahf*, 46.

[64] *Āl ʿImrān*, 185.

13

Allah's Limitless and Fathomless
Knowledge

The next parable we will be exploring is found in verse 14 of *Sūrah Al-Ra'd*. This verse is preceded by an oft-recited passage of the Qur'an which illustrates Allah's ﷻ infinite knowledge and power. This passage informs us that Allah ﷻ knows what every female bears and what increases and decreases in the wombs. He knows whether the egg will be fertilised or not, whether the baby will be born before or after nine months, whether the pregnancy will end with delivery or miscarriage, and whether there will be one baby or more. He is the Knower of the seen and the unseen—the All-Great, Most Exalted.

Describing His all-encompassing knowledge, Allah ﷻ says,

سَوَاءٌ مِّنكُم مَّنْ أَسَرَّ الْقَوْلَ وَمَن جَهَرَ بِهِ وَمَنْ هُوَ مُسْتَخْفٍ بِاللَّيْلِ وَسَارِبٌ بِالنَّهَارِ

"It is the same [to Him] whether any of you speaks secretly or openly, whether one hides in the darkness of night or goes about in broad daylight." [65]

Allah ﷻ then says,

لَهُ مُعَقِّبَاتٌ مِّن بَيْنِ يَدَيْهِ وَمِنْ خَلْفِهِ يَحْفَظُونَهُ مِنْ أَمْرِ اللَّهِ

"For each one there are successive angels before and behind, protecting them by Allah's command." [66]

This is then followed by the famous statement,

إِنَّ اللَّهَ لَا يُغَيِّرُ مَا بِقَوْمٍ حَتَّىٰ يُغَيِّرُوا مَا بِأَنفُسِهِمْ

"Indeed, Allah would never change a people's state [of favour] until they change their own state [of faith]." [67]

This statement informs us that if any blessing is removed from us, then it is due to some shortcoming within us. Allah ﷻ does not remove a blessing from us, nor does He change our situation for the worse except by our own design.

---

[65] *Al-Raʿd*, 10.

[66] *Al-Raʿd*, 11.

[67] Ibid.

Allah ﷻ then says,

وَإِذَا أَرَادَ اللَّهُ بِقَوْمٍ سُوءًا فَلَا مَرَدَّ لَهُ ۚ وَمَا لَهُم مِّن دُونِهِ مِن وَالٍ

*"And if it is Allah's Will to torment a people,
it can never be averted, nor can they find a
protector other than Him."* [68]

Further on, Allah ﷻ mentions that even the natural elements
glorify and praise Him,

هُوَ ٱلَّذِى يُرِيكُمُ ٱلْبَرْقَ خَوْفًا وَطَمَعًا وَيُنشِئُ ٱلسَّحَابَ ٱلثِّقَالَ .
وَيُسَبِّحُ ٱلرَّعْدُ بِحَمْدِهِ وَٱلْمَلَـٰئِكَةُ مِنْ خِيفَتِهِۦ

*"He is the One Who shows you lightning, inspiring
[you with] hope and fear, and produces heavy clouds.
The thunder glorifies His praises, as do the
angels in awe of Him."* [69]

After this inspiring discourse, Allah ﷻ presents the parable,

لَهُ دَعْوَةُ الْحَقِّ

"To Him belongs da'wah al-ḥaqq." [70]

---

[68] Ibid.

[69] *Al-Ra'd*, 12-13.

[70] *Al-Ra'd*, 14.

This statement, in particular the phrase da'wah al-ḥaqq, can be interpreted in two ways,

1. **"To Him [alone] is the call of truth."**

   According to this interpretation, even though the verse is apparently about du'ā' (supplication), Allah ﷻ uses the word da'wah (call). This would mean that to Allah ﷻ belongs the call of truth; that Allah's ﷻ da'wah is the true da'wah. What is Allah's ﷻ da'wah? Ibn 'Abbās ؓ said that Allah's ﷻ da'wah is lā ilāha illa Allāh.

2. **"Calling upon Him [alone] is the truth."**

   According to this interpretation, calling out to Allah ﷻ in supplication (du'ā') is a supplication of truth. We should supplicate only to Allah ﷻ and no one else, for this is the truth and a fundamental of our faith. Any person that does otherwise has transgressed and violated the exclusive right of Allah ﷻ. Allah ﷻ says in the Qur'an,

   وَأَنَّ الْمَسَاجِدَ لِلَّهِ فَلَا تَدْعُوا مَعَ اللَّهِ أَحَدًا

   "The places of worship are [only] for Allah, so do not invoke anyone besides Him." [71]

---

[71] *Al-Jinn,* 18.

After mention of the *da'wah al-ḥaqq*, Allah ﷻ continues by presenting this parable,

وَالَّذِينَ يَدْعُونَ مِن دُونِهِ لَا يَسْتَجِيبُونَ لَهُم بِشَيْءٍ إِلَّا كَبَاسِطِ كَفَّيْهِ
إِلَى الْمَاءِ لِيَبْلُغَ فَاهُ وَمَا هُوَ بِبَالِغِهِ ۚ وَمَا دُعَاءُ الْكَافِرِينَ إِلَّا فِي ضَلَالٍ

"But those [idols] the pagans invoke besides Him [can] never respond to them in any way. [It is] just like someone who stretches out their hands to water, [asking it] to reach their mouths, but it can never do so. The calls of the disbelievers are only in vain."[72]

Supplicating to other than Allah ﷻ is bereft of benefit and will not aid you in attaining anything, not even partially. Thus, the pagan practice of invoking idols was fruitless, and Allah ﷻ is presenting a parable to demonstrate this futility. Allah ﷻ compares such pagans to a thirsty desert wanderer who sees a mirage, so he stretches his hands out towards the mirage, inanely thinking that by doing so water will miraculously come into his mouth. This is despite the water he is seeking being non-existent and a figment of his imagination. Similarly, the stretching of the hands towards idols—which is a symbol of invocation because every faith has some involvement of the hand whilst supplicating—is futile as the idols do not truly exist as a source of benefit. Furthermore, even if the water was part of a real oasis, stretching his hands out from afar would not be sufficient, as he would have to

---

[72] *Al-Ra'd*, 14.

physically go and gather water into his hands by the oasis. By this, Allah ﷻ is indicating that even if existent entities apart from Him are invoked, such as ʿĪsā ﷺ or any other Prophet ﷺ, this is still futile. The answer to such an invocation will never reach them, as the prayer of the disbelievers made to false entities is nothing but straying in void.

This parable is powerful as it paints the picture that someone who invokes other than Allah ﷻ has completely lost their senses. Invoking other than Allah ﷻ is a grand delusion, for there is absolutely no benefit in doing so, and you will receive nothing for it. To Allah ﷻ and Allah ﷻ alone supplication is made, for this is the only supplication that can benefit.

14

The Eternal Truth
Prevails Against Falsehood

We previously explored the powerful linguistic device found in *Sūrah al-Baqarah*, where Allah ﷻ presents opposite concepts in the parables mentioning the kindling of fire and descending rain. Similarly, in verse 17 of *Sūrah al-Ra'd*, Allah ﷻ again presents two parables of opposite concepts embedded within one verse. Giving such contrasting parables is part of the methodology of the Qur'an due to the piercing effects of this linguistic device.

Allah ﷻ says,

أَنزَلَ مِنَ السَّمَاءِ مَاءً فَسَالَتْ أَوْدِيَةٌ بِقَدَرِهَا

"He sends down rain from the sky, causing the valleys to flow, each according to its capacity." [73]

---

[73] *Al-Ra'd*, 17.

This parable creates the mental image of rain falling from the sky upon mountains during the monsoon season. The dry mountain valleys that are usually empty become filled with water during this season, brimming to the edge in accordance with the size of each individual valley.

$$\text{فَٱحْتَمَلَ ٱلسَّيْلُ زَبَدًا رَّابِيًا}$$

"The currents then carry along rising scum"

As the rainwater gushes down into the valleys, scum is carried along. This valueless scum includes leaves, twigs, and various other flotsam and jetsam which are all covered by the produced froth of the waves. This is a holistic mental image that Allah ﷻ intends to create.

Immediately thereafter, Allah ﷻ mentions a related parable regarding fire,

$$\text{وَمِمَّا يُوقِدُونَ عَلَيْهِ فِي ٱلنَّارِ ٱبْتِغَاءَ حِلْيَةٍ أَوْ مَتَاعٍ زَبَدٌ مِّثْلُهُ}$$

"Similar to the slag produced from metal that people melt in the fire for ornaments or tools."

Just as residues of scum and froth are produced as a result of water flow in mountain valleys, residues of slag are produced in a furnace when raw materials such as gold or silver are placed into it.

After reading these two parables, we are left wondering of their relevance, and the key message that Allah ﷻ is attempting to deliver to us through them. Clarifying this, Allah ﷻ says:

كَذَٰلِكَ يَضْرِبُ اللَّهُ الْحَقَّ وَالْبَاطِلَ

"This is how Allah compares truth to falsehood."

These parables give us an example of truth versus falsehood. How is this done?

فَأَمَّا الزَّبَدُ فَيَذْهَبُ جُفَاءً

"The [worthless] residue is then cast away."

The valueless upper residue of the flowing valley water and furnace will eventually be rid of and cast away, even if it may originally seem like an alluring and integral part of the water flow.

وَأَمَّا مَا يَنْفَعُ النَّاسَ فَيَمْكُثُ فِي الْأَرْضِ

"But what benefits people remains on the earth."

As for that which benefits mankind from the flowing water and furnace, this is what will remain.

In this parable, Allah ﷻ is comparing rain to the Guiding Qur'an. This divine revelational rain descends upon the valleys of peoples' hearts. Similar to valleys, as each heart is unique in terms of depth, width, and absorption, the reaction to having this divine rain poured upon it will differ from heart to heart. Some hearts will fully absorb to the brim, some will slightly absorb, and some will not absorb any water at all. This is corroborated by a Hadith in *Ṣaḥīḥ al-Bukhārī*, where it is mentioned that the Prophet ﷺ said,

"The example of that which Allah has sent me with is like that of descending rain. Some soils are fertile so it will absorb the rain, whilst other soils are flat and barren so it will reject the rain."

As for the residue of scum and slag, this represents the people who reject the truth and use Islam only to bring attention to themselves. This includes the hypocrites, the leaders of the disbelievers, or even insincere Muslims who misuse and exploit Islam for their own personal gain. They may originally seem to be at the top just like the scum and slag upon the water and furnace, but in the end, they will be the ones discarded and rid of just like these valueless residues. This is exactly what happens when water descends from the mountains into streams; the pure water proceeds to reach the beneficiaries, whilst the residues are left behind. This is similar to what occurs in a furnace. For when you put your raw material into the furnace the valueless residue first becomes apparent before eventually being expelled, leaving you with valuable pure gold or silver.

The main message we can derive from these metaphors and parables is that the ultimate truth will always eventually prevail, even if falsehood may be on top for a period of time. We should never be deluded by the evil or pretenders that may seem to be dominant, for eventually they will be discarded and swept away, leaving the shining truth to prevail.

Another important message we can extract from these parables is the importance of remaining firm and consistent.

وَأَمَّا مَا يَنفَعُ النَّاسَ فَيَمْكُثُ فِي الْأَرْضِ ۚ كَذَلِكَ يَضْرِبُ اللَّهُ الْأَمْثَالَ

"What benefits people remains on the earth.
This is how Allah sets forth parables."

We should not be worried about the temporary supremacy of evil, as only what is beneficial will eventually remain. We need to be firm, consistent, and not worry about these temporary circumstances. If we keep steadfast, we will remain upon the purity of the truth and become eventual sources of benefit for others.

Another point we can extract from this parable is that the scorching hot furnace can be compared to worldly tests. If a believer is firm and steadfast, he walks through this furnace and comes out like pure gold or silver, having been purified. Therefore, we should exercise forbearance upon being tested in this world. Be patient and hope for reward upon being criticised and mocked for your religiosity and unwavering faith.

Take courage from the divine revelation of Allah ﷻ and connect with your Creator through worship and study. If we do so, we will be from amongst the successful ones for whom the truth will remain dominant, while falsehood will be overcome. Reflect on the promise of Allah ﷻ,

وَالْعَاقِبَةُ لِلْمُتَّقِينَ

"The ultimate outcome belongs [only] to the righteous." [74]

[74] *Al-Aʿrāf*, 128.

15

The Necessity of
Being Grateful and
Thankful to Allah

In this chapter, we will explore one of the most common phrases that we hear in lectures and lessons. Allah ﷻ says,

$$لَئِن شَكَرْتُمْ لَأَزِيدَنَّكُمْ$$

"If you are grateful, I will certainly give you more."[75]

This is one of the most powerful and succinct summaries of the entire religion. In fact, the preceding part of the same verse is just as powerful,

$$وَإِذْ تَأَذَّنَ رَبُّكُمْ$$

"And [remember] when your Lord proclaimed"

[75] *Ibrāhīm, 7.*

Allah ﷻ has made a proclamation at the beginning of time. What is that proclamation?

لَئِن شَكَرْتُمْ لَأَزِيدَنَّكُمْ ۖ وَلَئِن كَفَرْتُمْ إِنَّ عَذَابِي لَشَدِيدٌ

"If you are grateful, I will certainly give you more. But if you are ungrateful, surely My punishment is severe."

This verse talks about the concept of thankfulness (*shukr*). We must understand this, and identify its blessings and methods because thanking Allah ﷻ is the very purpose of our creation,

اِنَّا هَدَيْنٰهُ السَّبِيلَ اِمَّا شَاكِرًا وَّاِمَّا كَفُورًا

"We already showed them the Way, whether they [choose to] be grateful or ungrateful." [76]

This verse informs us that the opposite of thankfulness (*shukr*) is rejection (*kufr*). Man can choose either of these ways, and this verse warns us against choosing *kufr*. We also learn from this verse that the true reality and essence of *kufr* is ungratefulness. This is why a disbeliever is called a *kāfir*, as he is showing ungratefulness by rejecting All-Bountiful Allah ﷻ. Ungratefulness lies at the core of disbelief. On the contrary, the essence of faith (*īmān*) is to be thankful to Allah ﷻ for all the bounties and favours He blessed us with. In fact, He blessed us with all of these things in order for

[76] *Al-Insān*, 3.

us to show thanks to Him. When the Prophet Sulaymān
was blessed immensely, he said,

$$قَالَ هَٰذَا مِن فَضْلِ رَبِّي لِيَبْلُوَنِي أَأَشْكُرُ أَمْ أَكْفُرُ$$

"He exclaimed, 'This is by the grace of my Lord to
test me whether I am grateful or ungrateful.'"[77]

We should think of this prophetic statement every time we
look at the blessings which Allah ﷻ has given us, such as our
families and wealth. It is all from Allah ﷻ,

$$لِيَبْلُوَنِي أَأَشْكُرُ أَمْ أَكْفُرُ$$

"To test me whether I am grateful or ungrateful."

Allah ﷻ also tells us in the Qur'an,

$$وَ اللهُ أَخْرَجَكُم مِّنْ بُطُونِ أُمَّهَٰتِكُمْ لَا تَعْلَمُونَ شَيْئًا وَّجَعَلَ$$
$$لَكُمُ السَّمْعَ وَ الْأَبْصَارَ وَ الْأَفْئِدَةَ$$

"And Allah brought you out of the wombs of your mothers
while you knew nothing, and gave you hearing,
sight, and intellect..."[78]

---

[77] *Al-Naml*, 40.

[78] *Al-Naḥl*, 78.

لَعَلَّكُمْ تَشْكُرُونَ

"So perhaps you would be thankful"

The reason for being blessed in this world is subsequently thankfulness. This is the very essence of creation.

We must also learn how to be properly thankful to Allah ﷻ. Ibn al-Qayyim has a beautiful passage in *Madārij al-Sālikīn*, where he mentions that *shukr* is done in multiple ways,

1. *Shukr* is done by firmly acknowledging that Allah ﷻ has given you all that you have and that nothing is truly from you, your abilities, or your actions.

2. Such acknowledgement should lead to humility, appreciation, and a genuine sense of thankfulness to Allah ﷻ in your heart.

3. The feeling should then move from the heart to the tongue, leading it to begin praising Allah ﷻ, glorifying Him, and verbally thanking Him for His endowments.

4. The *shukr* should then cause you to be appreciative in your actions, rituals, and worship.

5. Any special blessings that Allah ﷻ has bestowed upon you should be used in the service of Allah ﷻ, such as abundant wealth or authority. This is an ultimate sign

of *shukr*: that you use the blessing to worship Allah ﷻ and not to disobey Him. Allah ﷻ said to Dāwūd and Sulaymān ﷺ,

$$اعْمَلُوا آلَ دَاوُدَ شُكْراً$$

"Work gratefully, O family of Dāwūd!"

This was said to them since in addition to Prophethood, they were also blessed with the rare bounties of kingship and dominion. They had the choicest blessings of this world and the Hereafter as both Prophets and Kings, so Allah ﷻ instructed them to show gratefulness in their actions. It is interesting to note that our Prophet ﷺ was also offered kingship by Allah ﷻ via Jibrīl ﷺ, but he refused.

We learn from these above points that *shukr* is made on the tongue, felt in the heart, and exhibited in actions and rituals.

If we make *shukr* in the above-mentioned ways, The Qur'an mentions many benefits that we will gain,

1. When we are thankful, Allah ﷻ protects us from punishments. Thus, collective punishments are a sign that we have been ungrateful and unthankful, and are reminders for us to reorient ourselves in return to Allah ﷻ. In light of new pandemics such as COVID-19, we need to deeply reflect on this point. Allah ﷻ says in the Qur'an,

مَا يَفْعَلُ اللّٰهُ بِعَذَابِكُمْ إِنْ شَكَرْتُمْ وَآمَنْتُمْ

*"Why should Allah punish you if you are
grateful and faithful?"*[79]

2. Allah ﷻ tells us in the verse that He will give us more if
   we are thankful, for His treasures can never be depleted.

لَئِنْ شَكَرْتُمْ لَأَزِيدَنَّكُمْ

"If you are grateful, I will certainly give you more."

3. The final and best benefit is that Allah ﷻ will be pleased
   with us, which is the greatest achievement for a person.
   Allah ﷻ says,

وَإِنْ تَشْكُرُوا يَرْضَهُ لَكُمْ

"If you are grateful, He is pleased [to see] it in you."[80]

Let us now explore some practical tips to be thankful about
as per prophetic guidance.

1. First and foremost, our Prophet ﷺ said to look to people
   who have less than you in order to feel thankfulness. One
   of the obsessions of western culture is to always look at

---

79 *Al-Nisā'*, 147.

80 *Al-Zumar*, 39.

111

the lifestyles of the most elite, influential, famous, and excessively rich people in society. People obsess over the top one per cent of people on the wealth and influence scale. We should not look at such individuals, as this will lead to insecurity. Rather, the Prophet  instructed us to look at those we have been blessed over in the world. Look at those who are struggling, the homeless, the orphans, the refugees, and then praise Allah ﷻ that you have a roof over your head and sufficient means. Make a habit of constantly repeating the statement *alḥamdu-lillāh* (all praises are due to Allah)!

2. In a Hadith of Tirmidhī, the Prophet ﷺ said,

$$\text{كُنْ قَنِعًا تَكُنْ أَشْكَرَ النَّاسِ}$$

"Be content, and you will be the most grateful of people [to Allah]."

If you are content and happy with your health, family, wealth, and whatever else you have without holding any greed in your heart, you are the most grateful of people.

3. Our Prophet ﷺ advised that we should supplicate to Allah ﷻ for aid in thanking Him. In the famous Hadith, we are informed that the Prophet ﷺ once took hold of the hand of Muʿādh ibn Jabal ﷺ and said to him,

"O Mu'ādh! I swear by Allah that I most definitely love you, I swear by Allah that I most definitely love you." He then said *"I advise you—O Mu'ādh— that you be sure not to leave out saying the following at the end of every prayer:*

اللَّهُمَّ أَعِنِّي عَلَى ذِكْرِكَ وَشُكْرِكَ وَحُسْنِ عِبَادَتِكَ

O Allah! Assist me in remembering You, being grateful to You, and worshipping You in a beautiful manner."

4. Our Prophet ﷺ also said that if you want to be thankful to Allah, then thank the people who have helped you. For if you do not thank the people, you are in fact arrogant. Thanking those that help you will give you humility, and you will see that Allah is using so many people to bring good and blessings to you. Our Prophet ﷺ said,

"He who does not thank people [who have assisted him] is not thankful to Allah."

We pray that Allah ﷻ makes us amongst the thankful, and allows us to follow the Sunnah in doing so.

16

True Faith Manifested:
The Parable of the Good Tree

The parable found in verse 24 of *Sūrah Ibrāhīm* is a celebrated and renowned Qur'anic parable. It is a personal favourite of mine and upon which I have given many hundreds of lectures around the world. In fact, the first lecture I ever delivered was regarding this parable. This is due to its profound nature. In fact, Allah ﷻ begins the parable with a rhetorical question in order to emphasise that we must reflect upon it carefully. Allah ﷻ says,

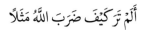

"Have you not seen how Allah has set forth a parable?" [81]

---

[81] *Ibrāhīm*, 24.

This is the only parable in the Noble Qur'an that begins with Allah ﷻ drawing our attention in such a way. Similarly, at the end of the parable, Allah ﷻ says,

$$وَيَضْرِبُ اللَّهُ الْأَمْثَالَ لِلنَّاسِ لَعَلَّهُمْ يَتَذَكَّرُونَ$$

"This is how Allah sets forth parables for the people, so perhaps they will be mindful."[82]

Allah ﷻ is drawing extra attention to this parable both at its beginning and end, which is an unprecedented feature of it.

$$أَلَمْ تَرَ كَيْفَ ضَرَبَ اللَّهُ مَثَلًا$$

"Have you not seen how Allah has set forth a parable?"

$$كَلِمَةً طَيِّبَةً كَشَجَرَةٍ طَيِّبَةٍ أَصْلُهَا ثَابِتٌ وَفَرْعُهَا فِي السَّمَاءِ$$

"A good word is like a good tree whose root is firm and whose branches are high in the sky"[83]

This particular parable can be examined from two paradigms. As for the first, Ibn ʿAbbās ﷺ is of the opinion that the 'good word' (*kalimah ṭayyibah*) is the statement *lā ilāha illa Allāh*. Therefore, this is a parable of the oneness of Allah (*tawḥīd*)—the core of our faith and religion.

---

[82] *Ibrāhīm*, 25.

[83] *Ibrāhīm*, 24.

كَلِمَةً طَيِّبَةً كَشَجَرَةٍ طَيِّبَةٍ أَصْلُهَا ثَابِتٌ وَفَرْعُهَا فِي السَّمَاءِ

"A good word [lā ilāha illa Allāh] is like
a good tree whose root is firm and whose
branches are high in the sky" [84]

The words *lā ilāha illa Allāh* are like a beautiful and magnificent tree, which is universally seen as a symbol of life across
societies and cultures. Also from a biological perspective,
a tree is a basic building block of life. During primary
education, one of the first lessons taught to children studying
biology is regarding trees and the process of photosynthesis,
due to its integral role in the sustaining of life. Trees take in
carbon dioxide (from the air), water (from the ground), and
light (usually from the sun). Eventually the carbon dioxide
and water are converted into oxygen, which is then released
into the air. We will not be able to live without the oxygen
produced by trees, as we require it to breathe. The trees also
give us fire with which we burn our fuel and cook our food.
The trees also shelter us and provide us with wood. We are to
a great extent dependent on trees for our livelihood; we eat,
drink, breathe, and live because of the trees. Without trees,
there is quite possibly no tenable life on this earth. Similarly,
without *lā ilāha illa Allāh* there is no life in the heart and
the spiritual soul will be dead.

---

[84] *Ibrāhīm*, 24.

$$ كَلِمَةً طَيِّبَةً كَشَجَرَةٍ طَيِّبَةٍ $$

"A good word [lā ilāha illa Allāh] is like a good tree."

Lā ilāha illa Allāh is not any old tree, but it is a beautiful and magnificent tree. It is a tree that pleases the onlooker.

$$ أَصْلُهَا ثَابِتٌ $$

"Whose root is firm"

The roots of the tree of *lā ilāha illa Allāh* are not shallow. Rather, the roots go very deep. This is the reality of true faith—when it genuinely enters the heart, it can never leave after that. This is why Muslims around the world are by and large faithful to their religion. Statistics indicate that the belief in God in Muslim majority countries is skyrocketing whilst the exact opposite is happening in European countries, where only twenty to forty per cent of people truly believe in God and adhere to religion. *Alḥamdulillāh*, in Muslim majority lands, seventy to ninety per cent of Muslims practise the rituals of their faith—much more than any other religion. In fact, the most observed ritual on the entire globe is the fast of Ramadan. No ritual of any other religion can compete in terms of the number of people practising one ritual in unison. This is due to the deep roots of *lā ilāha illa Allāh*, entrenching faith firmly inside our hearts. This is also demonstrated in the reality that many people revert to Islam, whilst the number of converts to other religions is utterly insignificant in comparison. Intellectuals, teachers, preachers, and people from all walks of life embrace our religion. We find great minds of Christianity, Judaism, and other faiths and traditions embracing Islam, whilst no intellectual Islamic scholar or learned man abandoned Islam in favour of other creeds such as Christianity or Buddhism in our entire history. This is not to say that we do not have a problem of youth apostasy; however, many are becoming agnostics due to firm faith not having entered their hearts previously. They are born in Muslim households, but have not tasted the sweetness of faith due to environmental and other factors. The reality is that those who taste the real sweetness of faith can never apostatise. Muslims may slip up and commit sins, but if they have truly tasted faith, they will never abandon it. Despite incessantly sinning, deep down inside every Muslim there is an inner realisation of the evil of their sins: this is the deep-rooted faith that tells them that Allah is merciful, and this will drive them to eventual repentance. That is the reality of faith that we understand from the Hadith of *Ṣaḥīḥ al-Bukhārī*, that describes the scene when Abū Sufyān was questioned about the Prophet ﷺ before Hercules, the Caesar of Rome. One of the questions asked was regarding if anyone had apostatised from the faith of this man, to which Abū Sufyān honestly replied in the negative. This was astounding as it was in the Meccan period when people were being brutally persecuted and tortured, yet never was there a case of an apostate from Islam in Makkah. This was due to the deep-rooted faith of the believers.

$$\text{وَفَرْعُهَا فِي السَّمَاءِ}$$

"Whose branches are high in the sky"

Not only is the tree of *lā ilāha illa Allāh* deep-rooted, but it is also towering high in the sky. It is like the massive and mighty trees found in forests such as the Redwood Forest in California. In fact, the tree of *lā ilāha illa Allāh* is taller than even those trees, as its branches reach all the way to the heavens. It is so huge that it is impossible to hide; no skyscraper or building can block it. This is the reality of the tree of faith; it is so tall that it lifts you all the way to Paradise. All can physically see it, for when faith exists in the heart it exhibits itself on the outer limbs. It is visible in your actions, behaviour, and social interactions. Just as people look up at and admire the landmark tree, people will look up to and admire the one who possesses the tree of faith and will take that person as a role model. Those who possess the tree of *lā ilāha illa Allāh* will be raised,

$$\text{يَرْفَعِ اللَّهُ الَّذِينَ آمَنُوا مِنكُمْ وَالَّذِينَ أُوتُوا الْعِلْمَ دَرَجَاتٍ}$$

"Allah will elevate those of you who are faithful, and [raise] those gifted with knowledge in rank." [85]

___

[85] *Al-Mujādilah*, 11.

Continuing with the parable, Allah ﷻ says,

$$ تُؤْتِىٓ أُكُلَهَا كُلَّ حِينٍ بِإِذْنِ رَبِّهَا ۗ $$

*"[Always] yielding its fruit in every season
by the Will of its Lord."* [86]

The tree of *lā ilāha illa Allāh* is evergreen and ever fruitful, always ready to be plucked from and still increasing its yield. It has whatever a person needs and desires. This tree gives not only one fruit but multiple fruits throughout the seasons, which is understood from the usage of the Arabic plural for the fruits, *'ukul'*. Thus, when you require perseverance (*ṣabr*), the tree of faith will give you it. When you require an increase in reliance (*tawakkul*) and conviction (*yaqīn*), the tree of faith will give you it. When you are feeling down or lonely, the tree of faith will cheer you up and give you company. Whatever type of sustenance or glucose you need at any time, the tree of faith will certainly have the required fruit throughout the seasons. Over 25 fruits have been mentioned in the Qur'an. From amongst them is peace in this world, happiness, strength of faith, confidence and conviction, meeting death with *lā ilāha illa Allāh* upon the tongue, protection from the torment of the grave, salvation on the Day of Judgement, and most importantly entering Paradise and seeing Allah ﷻ.

THE PARABLES OF THE QURAN

[86] *Ibrāhīm*, 25.

These are the fruits exclusively available from the tree of faith, and are unique to it. This is all by the will and permission of its Lord.

وَيَضْرِبُ اللَّهُ الْأَمْثَالَ لِلنَّاسِ لَعَلَّهُمْ يَتَذَكَّرُونَ

"This is how Allah sets forth parables for the people, so perhaps they will be mindful."

May Allah ﷻ make us from the mindful ones.

17

Faith Verses Falsehood: Exploring the Parables of the Good and Evil Trees

In the previous chapter, we explored the beautiful parable found in verse 24 of *Sūrah Ibrāhīm* from one paradigm. According to this paradigm, as mentioned by Ibn ʿAbbās ☙, the 'good word' (*kalimah ṭayyibah*) is the statement *lā ilāha illa Allāh*—having firm faith by testifying to the oneness of Allah.

أَلَمۡ تَرَ كَيۡفَ ضَرَبَ اللَّهُ مَثَلًا

"Have you not seen how Allah has set forth a parable?"

كَلِمَةً طَيِّبَةً كَشَجَرَةٍ طَيِّبَةٍ أَصۡلُهَا ثَابِتٌ وَفَرۡعُهَا فِي السَّمَاءِ

"A good word is like a good tree whose root is firm and whose branches are high in the sky" [87]

---

[87] *Ibrāhīm*, 24.

In this chapter, we will explore this parable from a second paradigm that has been presented by many scholars, such as Ibn al-Jawzī ﷺ and the famous exegete Ibn 'Āshūr. They posit that the 'good word' (*kalimah ṭayyibah*) is the good speech of Allah ﷻ Himself—the Qur'an. Thus, the Qur'an is like a beautiful tree that roots itself deeper in the heart the more it is recited, causing faith and love for the Qur'an to exponentially grow.

أَصْلُهَا ثَابِتٌ

"Whose root is firm"

وَفَرْعُهَا فِي السَّمَاءِ

"Whose branches are high in the sky"

As indicated in this verse, the Qur'an will raise a person up through its high and lofty branches. The Prophet ﷺ also said in this regard,

"Verily, Allah raises some people by this book, and by it He humbles others."

We also learn from the Hadith in *Ṣaḥīḥ al-Bukhārī* that our Prophet ﷺ mentioned that on the Day of Judgment the companion of the Qur'an (*ṣāḥib al-Qur'an*) will be told to recite and rise, elevating by one rank for every verse he recites. This shows us that the concept of rising due to the Qur'an is an authentically established concept from the Qur'an and Sunnah. Allah ﷺ then says,

$$تُؤْتِي أُكُلَهَا كُلَّ حِينٍ بِإِذْنِ رَبِّهَا$$

"[always] yielding its fruit in every season
by the Will of its Lord."[88]

The Qur'an blesses us with its varied and delectable fruits in all seasons. Whenever we are feeling sad or depressed; whenever we are being tested and require assistance upon patience; whenever the world is weighing down upon our shoulders and we do not know how much further we can persist; whenever situations seem bleak; whenever we require anything at all; on all such occasions turn to the Qur'an, recite the Qur'an, seek assistance through the Qur'an, and gain inspiration and blessings from the Qur'an. The Qur'an is the one book that can certainly give you what you need.

In addition to the two previously mentioned explanations of the 'good word' (*kalimah ṭayyibah*), there is also a third interpretation presented by a small group of scholars. They opined that *kalimah ṭayyibah* is any beautiful and positive word, such as inviting somebody to Islam, following the Sunnah of being cheerful in your interactions, or sharing any other general good words or encouragement. All of these actions count as *kalimah ṭayyibah*, as you are planting

[88] *Ibrāhīm*, 25.

healthy seeds in people that will grow. They will develop into beautiful deep-rooted trees, with high and lofty branches that will continue to benefit others for generations to come. Thus, this interpretation is very general in its implication.

In summary, the first part of this parable that we have discussed has three valid interpretations,

1. *Kalimah ṭayyibah is lā ilāha illa Allāh*—this is the majority opinion.

2. *Kalimah ṭayyibah is the Qur'an*—an opinion supported by many scholars.

3. *Kalimah ṭayyibah is any good word*—the opinion of a small number of scholars.

None of these interpretations are mutually exclusive; in fact, they support one another. It is the Qur'an that teaches us *lā ilāha illa Allāh*, and *lā ilāha illa Allāh* is explained by the teachings of the Qur'an.

We now move on to the next part of the parable, which flips the example on its head. Allah ﷻ says,

وَمَثَلُ كَلِمَةٍ خَبِيثَةٍ كَشَجَرَةٍ خَبِيثَةٍ ٱجْتُثَّتْ مِن فَوْقِ ٱلْأَرْضِ مَا لَهَا مِن قَرَارٍ

"And the parable of an evil word is that of an evil tree, uprooted from the earth, having no stability."[89]

The interpretation of an 'evil word' (*kalimah khabīthah*) would depend on how the 'good word' (*kalimah ṭayyibah*) was defined.

1. If the *kalimah ṭayyibah* is *lā ilāha illa Allāh*, then the *kalimah khabīthah* is any word calling to association of partners with Allah (*shirk*).

2. If the *kalimah ṭayyibah* is interpreted as the Qur'an, then the *kalimah khabīthah* is any speech, ideology, or methodology used to reject the Qur'an.

In the parable, Allah ﷻ likens the *kalimah khabīthah* to an evil tree that is thorny and prickly, having no beneficial leaves, flowers, or fruits. Nobody likes to see such a tree, as it is ugly to look at.

89 *Ibrāhīm*, 26.

ٱجۡتُثَّتۡ مِن فَوۡقِ ٱلۡأَرۡضِ

"Uprooted from the earth"

The roots of this tree have been pulled up from the surface of the earth; thus, the tree is tottering. Such a tree will not provide you stability in your life, as it is not properly anchored.

مَا لَهَا مِن قَرَارٍ

"Having no stability."

The state of this unsightly and tottering tree contrasts with the tree of *kalimah ṭayyibah*, which stands mightily tall and strong. This example makes it clear to mankind which tree they should aim to possess. When you have the strong tree of *kalimah ṭayyibah*, you will know your purpose in life and have the tools to deal with the trials and tribulations of life. Your faith is rock solid and will not be moved by the winds of falsehood. You will have stability in your life. On the other hand, when you do not possess the *kalimah ṭayyibah*, you are like uprooted and unsightly bushes that are not implanted in the earth. When the winds of falsehood come, you will be blown away and deposited wherever the winds decide to drop you. You have no stability, purpose, direction, or peace. You are like agricultural waste that has no value and is disposed of.

Allah  then says,

$$يُثَبِّتُ اللّٰهُ الَّذِيْنَ اٰمَنُوْا بِالْقَوْلِ الثَّابِتِ فِى الْحَيٰوةِ الدُّنْيَا وَفِى الْاٰخِرَةِ$$

"Allah makes the believers steadfast with the firm Word in this worldly life and the Hereafter."[90]

The 'firm word' (*al-qawl al-thābit*) is either *lā ilāha illa Allāh* or the Qur'an, depending on the interpretation of *kalimah ṭayyibah*. With this firm word, Allah ﷻ will make the believers steadfast in this world and the Hereafter.

$$فِى الْحَيٰوةِ الدُّنْيَا وَفِى الْاٰخِرَةِ$$

"In this worldly life and the Hereafter"

Ibn 'Abbās ﵁ said that the 'worldly life' refers to Allah ﷻ blessing a person to say *lā ilāha illa Allāh* at the time of leaving this world. Our Prophet ﷺ said that whoever's last words are *lā ilāha illa Allāh* shall enter Paradise. May Allah ﷻ make this the last phrase we say. We can aim to guarantee this by remaining firm upon the *kalimah ṭayyibah*, for Allah ﷻ informs us that if we are loyal to it, He will make it firm for us. As for in the 'Hereafter', Ibn 'Abbās ﵁ said when the angels of questioning (Munkar and Nakīr) come to you in the grave and ask you the three decisive questions, Allah ﷻ will support you with the correct answers.

---

90 *Ibrāhīm*, 27.

In conclusion, after reflecting on these two powerful parables, we should be motivated to be amongst those whom Allah will affirm and strengthen in this world and the Hereafter. In order to achieve this, we should say *lā ilāha illa Allāh*, study *lā ilāha illa Allāh*, turn to *lā ilāha illa Allāh*, recite the Qur'an, memorise the Qur'an, and learn the Qur'an. If we do so, Allah ﷻ will make us firm, enable us to say *lā ilāha illa Allāh* when we leave this world, and support us in answering the questions of the grave. May Allah ﷻ grant us that.

18

The Theological Absurdities and Contradictions of **Polytheism**

In this chapter, we will cover multiple parables of a similar motif. The first two are found in verses 75 and 76 of *Sūrah al-Naḥl*, where Allah ﷻ gives two parables,

ضَرَبَ ٱللَّهُ مَثَلًا عَبْدًا مَّمْلُوكًا لَّا يَقْدِرُ عَلَىٰ شَىْءٍ وَمَن رَّزَقْنَٰهُ مِنَّا رِزْقًا حَسَنًا فَهُوَ يُنفِقُ مِنْهُ سِرًّا وَجَهْرًا ۚ هَلْ يَسْتَوُۥنَ ۚ ٱلْحَمْدُ لِلَّهِ ۚ بَلْ أَكْثَرُهُمْ لَا يَعْلَمُونَ

"Allah sets forth a parable: a slave who lacks all means, compared to a [free] man to whom We granted a good provision, of which he donates [freely,] openly and secretly. Are they equal? [91]

---

[91] *Al-Naḥl*, 75.

Allah ﷻ compares an impoverished slave to an affluent free man who Allah ﷻ has blessed immensely. Allah ﷻ then poses a question,

"Are they equal?"

This parable has two interpretations according to our scholars, which in reality complement each other and can be carried across to other verses too. The first interpretation is that the righteous Muslim is being compared to the one who does not believe in Allah ﷻ. Accordingly, Allah ﷻ is saying that the one who is stingy, owns nothing, and spends nothing is not equal to someone who is wealthy and spends for the sake of Allah ﷻ. The second interpretation—which is the primary and higher interpretation according to the majority of scholars due to the context of the chapter revolving around the conflict of idolatry with *tawḥīd*—is that Allah ﷻ is relating a parable regarding Himself. Can the One who is all powerful and spends, i.e. Allah ﷻ, be equal to the ones who are incompetent and have nothing to spend, i.e. the false gods? Are they the same?

In the very next verse, Allah ﷻ presents the next parable,

وَضَرَبَ اللَّهُ مَثَلًا رَّجُلَيْنِ أَحَدُهُمَا أَبْكَمُ لَا يَقْدِرُ عَلَىٰ شَيْءٍ وَهُوَ كَلٌّ عَلَىٰ
مَوْلَاهُ أَيْنَمَا يُوَجِّههُّ لَا يَأْتِ بِخَيْرٍ هَلْ يَسْتَوِي هُوَ وَمَن يَأْمُرُ بِالْعَدْلِ
وَهُوَ عَلَىٰ صِرَاطٍ مُّسْتَقِيمٍ

"And Allah sets forth a parable of two men: one of them is dumb, incapable of anything. He is a burden on his master. Wherever he is sent, he brings no good. Can such a person be equal to the one who commands justice and is on the Straight Path?"[92]

In this parable, the first person presented is an incapable servant unable to work due to handicaps, thus a burden on his owner. This represents a person who is burdensome on society, does not benefit anyone, and is unable to be a force for good. Can such a person be equal to the one who is standing firm as a proactive force in society by guiding others, commanding them towards good, teaching, and being a positive influence? Some scholars have mentioned particular names within these two categories of people, such as Umayyah ibn Khalaf and Abū Jahl as the incompetent ones, and Abū Bakr al-Ṣiddīq and Ḥamzah ﷺ as the good guides. The broader interpretation would be that this is a parable of the false gods versus Allah ﷻ. The false gods have no capabilities and are handicapped, being burdens on the very people who carved or purchased them. No matter

---

92 *Al-Naḥl*, 76.

how many offerings are devoted to the idol, the idol will not benefit anyone at all. Can that useless idol be equal to Allah *al-Hādī* (the Guide) 🌸, who commands good and calls to righteousness?

In summary, the parables found in *Sūrah an-Naḥl* verses 75 and 76 can be understood on both a human level and a divine level, as discussed.

The next parable we will be exploring is found in *Sūrah al-Rūm*,

$$ضَرَبَ لَكُم مَّثَلًا مِّنْ أَنفُسِكُمْ هَل لَّكُم مِّن مَّا مَلَكَتْ أَيْمَانُكُم مِّن شُرَكَاءَ فِي مَا رَزَقْنَاكُمْ فَأَنتُمْ فِيهِ سَوَاءٌ تَخَافُونَهُمْ كَخِيفَتِكُمْ أَنفُسَكُمْ كَذَلِكَ نُفَصِّلُ الْآيَاتِ لِقَوْمٍ يَعْقِلُونَ$$

"He sets forth for you an example [drawn] from your own lives: would you allow some of those [bondspeople] in your possession to be your equal partners in whatever [wealth] We have provided you, fearing them as you have fear of each other? This is how We make the signs clear for people who understand."[93]

Allah 🌸 says that He is presenting an example you are familiar with. Here, we should bear in mind that the Qur'an originally was revealed upon a society in which slavery was common and normal. Allah 🌸 is saying that these slaves that

---

[93] *Al-Rūm*, 28.

you own would never be regarded as equal partners to the respected and affluent owners. In order to understand this better in our context, we would say that if you are just a normal employee of a corporation, would you ever be regarded to be of equal level and status as the bosses and executives?

"Fearing them as you have fear of each other"

The metaphor is relaying that you have different strands of people in terms of socio-economic status, and each person is afforded different rights and privileges according to their status in society. A president or a major CEO will have higher privileges than others lower than them, and this is something that is well known and accepted. So, when you yourselves do not have a society where everything is completely equal, how can you then equate Allah ﷻ with these false gods! How can the created be equal to the Creator?

The final parable we will be exploring in this chapter is from
Sūrah al-Zumar,

$$\text{ضَرَبَ اللَّهُ مَثَلًا رَّجُلًا فِيهِ شُرَكَاءُ مُتَشَاكِسُونَ وَرَجُلًا سَلَمًا لِّرَجُلٍ}$$
$$\text{هَلْ يَسْتَوِيَانِ مَثَلًا ۚ الْحَمْدُ لِلَّهِ ۚ بَلْ أَكْثَرُهُمْ لَا يَعْلَمُونَ}$$

*"Allah sets forth the parable of a slave owned by several
quarrelsome masters, and a slave owned by only one
master. Are they equal in condition? Praise be to Allah!
In fact, most of them do not know."* [94]

Allah ﷻ has given the example of two slaves; one owned by
multiple people that are constantly quarrelling regarding
who he should serve, and the other owned by one content
master. It is similar to someone being employed by ten
different companies, with each company giving tasks and
work to the employee that cause a conflict of interest. The
companies then argue amongst themselves, as each have
a share in the employee and want him to complete their
work before the work of others, which in turn affects the
employee's productivity. On the other hand, we have a
productive employee with a single employer. Can they be
regarded as equal? In this parable, Allah ﷻ is asking how it
is possible that there can be multiple gods when the system
of this world is so perfect, running in faultless synchro-
nicity and harmony. It is also not possible that a person can

---

[94] *Al-Zumar*, 29.

be employed by ten corporations and stay productive in their own lives, so how can a person worship multiple gods?

Allah ﷻ tells us in the Qur'an,

$$\text{لَوْ كَانَ فِيهِمَآ اٰلِهَةٌ اِلَّا اللّٰهُ لَفَسَدَتَا}$$

"Had there been other gods besides Allah in the heavens or the earth, both [realms] would have surely been corrupted. So Glorified is Allah, Lord of the Throne, far above what they claim." [95]

If there were truly multiple gods in this world, then the world would be in chaos and disorder. It would not be in the state of harmony we see; everything has a synergy, has a symbiotic relationship, and is in perfect harmony. This indicates there is one Lord in control, one Master, one Ruler, and one Creator—Allah ﷻ. If He had partners or equals there would be chaos, just like there would be chaos and conflict if there were multiple leaders of any state with equal powers.

[95] *Al-Anbiyā'*, 72.

All of these above-mentioned parables reveal the same truth: there is only one Allah ﷻ with no partners or equals. We understand and realise this from our own relationships with other human beings. By observing the world around us, we certainly realise that there is but one God that we should worship.

$$\text{الْحَمْدُ لِلَّهِ ۚ بَلْ أَكْثَرُهُمْ لَا يَعْلَمُونَ}$$

"Praise be to Allah! In fact, most of them do not know."

May Allah ﷻ accept our efforts.

19

Building on One's Piety: The Danger of Returning to Sins

The parable explored in this chapter relates to the ending of actions. In verse 92 of *Sūrah al-Naḥl*, Allah ﷻ says,

وَلَا تَكُونُوا كَالَّتِي نَقَضَتْ غَزْلَهَا مِن بَعْدِ قُوَّةٍ أَنكَاثًا

"Do not be like the woman who [foolishly] unravels her yarn after it is firmly spun."[96]

This is a profound parable. It describes a lady who spins her yarn into a strong rope, after which she then starts wasting her original efforts by unravelling it. Those familiar with the process of carpet weaving will appreciate how senseless this is, as traditional weaving is an arduous process that involves taking hardly visible thread from a silkworm, attaching

---

[96] *Al-Naḥl*, 92.

it to a spool, and slowly weaving the thread into an item. It is laborious work that can still be observed in many places across the world, such as Uzbekistan, where it can take up to a year in order to have one carpet or rug handspun. Now, imagine that after completing a handspun rug through such a laborious process, the weaver herself starts unravelling it and turning it back into the thin original yarn. This would be senseless and absurd. However, this is the exact parable which Allah ﷻ presents,

$$وَلَا تَكُونُواْ كَٱلَّتِي نَقَضَتْ غَزْلَهَا مِنۢ بَعْدِ قُوَّةٍ أَنكَٰثًا$$

"Do not be like the woman who [foolishly] unravels her yarn after it is firmly spun"

She unravels all of her spun yarn (*ghazl*). '*Ghazal*' can also mean a beautiful rope, from which the English word 'Gazelle' originates from. This is as the gazelle is also a beautiful animal. *Ghazal* poetry ('romantic' poetry) also takes its name from the same Arabic root, as it is regarded as a beautiful form of poetry.

Allah ﷻ is telling us that we should not be like this witless weaving lady. The metaphor is regarding doing good actions that weave a beautiful rope, and then unravelling this rope of ours with our own disobedience. For example, we weave a beautiful rope by worshipping Allah ﷻ dutifully during Ramadan and adopting a good daily routine of prayer, attending the houses of Allah ﷻ, and being charitable.

You have now built a solid foundation. However, if you were to go back to your old bad habits after Ramadan ends and abandon all the good you inculcated during the month, you have unravelled the rope with your own hands. You have become no different to the witless lady in the Qur'anic parable. Essentially, through this parable, Allah ﷻ is telling us to protect our investments and efforts. Everything you achieve is by Allah's ﷻ help, so do not ruin your achievements and regress. Rather, we should always be looking to progress and improve.

The Qur'an mentions many ways that we can destroy our own deeds. The most obvious is *kufr* and *shirk*, from which we seek Allah's ﷻ eternal refuge. Another way is by acting for other than Allah ﷻ, as ostentation destroys deeds. We must ensure sincerity of intention. Allah ﷻ mentions another thing that destroys deeds in the Qur'an,

يَٰٓأَيُّهَا ٱلَّذِينَ ءَامَنُوا۟ لَا تَرْفَعُوٓا۟ أَصْوَٰتَكُمْ فَوْقَ صَوْتِ ٱلنَّبِىِّ وَلَا تَجْهَرُوا۟ لَهُۥ بِٱلْقَوْلِ كَجَهْرِ بَعْضِكُمْ لِبَعْضٍ أَن تَحْبَطَ أَعْمَٰلُكُمْ وَأَنتُمْ لَا تَشْعُرُونَ

"O believers! Do not raise your voices above the voice of the Prophet, nor speak loudly to him as you do to one another, or your deeds will become void while you are unaware." [97]

[97] *Al-Ḥujurāt*, 2.

The exegetes explain this as meaning that you should not consider your positions or opinions more correct and suitable than the positions of the Qur'an and Sunnah. A Muslim should submit himself to the divine sources— the Qur'an and authentic Sunnah. Showing arrogance before these divine sources is one of the most dangerous ways for deeds to be annihilated. This message is reiterated elsewhere in the Qur'an, where Allah ﷻ says,

$$\text{يَٰٓأَيُّهَا ٱلَّذِينَ ءَامَنُواْ لَا تُبْطِلُواْ صَدَقَٰتِكُم بِٱلْمَنِّ وَٱلْأَذَىٰ}$$

"O believers! Do not waste your charity with reminders [of your generosity] or hurtful words."[98]

Another way that deeds are destroyed can be found in a Hadith of *Ṣaḥīḥ al-Bukhārī*, where our Prophet ﷺ said,

"Whoever intentionally misses 'Aṣr prayer, his deeds have been destroyed."

Our scholars explain that missing the 'Aṣr prayer wipes out all the good deeds of that day, no matter how many they may be. Bearing this in mind, we must be extremely careful not to miss any prayer. Scholars also mention that one of the ways that good deeds are diminished is if we stop practising something good that we were previously accustomed to. This would be as if you are leading a race, and then give up

141

---

[98] *Al-Baqarah*, 264.

and return to the start line. In a hadith of *Ṣaḥīḥ al-Bukhārī*, our Prophet ﷺ told one of his wives not to be like so and so who used to offer the nightly vigil (*tahajjud*) and later stopped doing so.

Therefore, we need to ensure steadfastness upon good. We may not be able to maintain the same worship levels as Ramadan year-round, but we should certainly try to maintain an appropriate portion of it and not abandon it completely. If we offer 90 minutes daily of supererogatory worship in Ramadan, then we should offer it 10 minutes daily for the rest of the year. We fast thirty days in Ramadan, so fast at least a few days for the rest of the year. If we give our yearly *zakāt* during Ramadan, give other amounts of small optional charity regularly throughout the year. Remember that the most beloved of all deeds in the sight of Allah ﷻ is that which is consistent, even if it is small. Think about the empty spots in your life in terms of rituals and shortcomings, and do what is reasonable for you to make yourself a better person. If we do so consistently, we will avoid being like the witless weaver.

Another final way that good deeds can be destroyed is by oppressing others, which is the context of this parable. Violating the rights of Allah ﷻ is a serious enough crime. However, we know that Allah ﷻ readily accepts repentance, as He is All-Forgiving and All-Merciful. But when you transgress against another creation of Allah ﷻ by usurping their rights, you are setting yourself up for a shock on the

Day of Retribution. On that day, those that you backbit, slandered, financially cheated, harmed, or hurt in any way will take revenge upon you by taking your good deeds. You may have thought that you came with heaps of good, but in reality, you will be bankrupted by those you violated, who will now claim your good deeds. Allah ﷻ is certainly All-Forgiving and All-Merciful, but fellow human beings will not exhibit forgiveness and mercy. They will likely take your good deeds in full measure. This is why our Prophet ﷺ advised that if any of you has oppressed another, they should solve it in this world before the Hereafter. Disputes of the world can be solved with wealth and words, but in the Hereafter wealth is not the currency. The currency of the Hereafter is good deeds; we do not have enough good deeds to be giving to other people.

We ask Allah ﷻ to allow these parables and messages of the Qur'an to impact us. May He make us amongst those who Allah ﷻ describes as rightly guided,

ٱلَّذِينَ يَسْتَمِعُونَ ٱلْقَوْلَ فَيَتَّبِعُونَ أَحْسَنَهُۥ ۚ أُوْلَٰٓئِكَ ٱلَّذِينَ هَدَىٰهُمُ ٱللَّهُ وَأُوْلَٰٓئِكَ هُمْ أُوْلُواْ ٱلْأَلْبَٰبِ

"Those who listen to what is said and follow the best of it, they are the ones Allah has guided, and those are people of understanding." [99]

[99] *Al-Zumar*, 18.

20

The Sublime and Symbolic Beauty of the Verse of Light

In this chapter, we will be exploring the Verse of Light (*Āyah al-Nūr*); our intellectual history indicates that this verse contains the most complex and profound parable in the entire Qur'an. Over fifty treatises have been written specifically about this verse, including the *Mishkāh al-Anwār* of Imam al-Ghazālī ﷺ. Allah ﷺ says,

اللَّهُ نُورُ السَّمَاوَاتِ وَالْأَرْضِ

"Allah is the Light of the heavens and the earth." [100]

This parable can be understood in an entire spectrum of ways, including philosophical, metaphysical, spiritual, and various other interpretations within mainstream orthodox exegesis.

---

[100] *Al-Nūr*, 35.

Despite the multiplicity of interpretations, we will present here just the basic narrative of Ibn 'Abbās ﷺ that is found in *Tafsīr al-Ṭabarī* and *Zād al-Masīr* of Ibn al-Jawzī. According to this one popular interpretation from the many, the Verse of Light contains a parable regarding the heart of our Prophet ﷺ.

اللَّهُ نُورُ السَّمَاوَاتِ وَالْأَرْضِ

"Allah is the Light of the heavens and the earth."

According to this opinion, the 'light' (*nūr*) refers to the One who guides to the light—Allah ﷻ. As seen in various parables of the Qur'an, light represents guidance, and Allah is the guiding light; thus, His speech is also light, His Prophet ﷺ is light, and His religion is light.

مَثَلُ نُورِهِ كَمِشْكَاةٍ فِيهَا مِصْبَاحٌ ـ الْمِصْبَاحُ فِي زُجَاجَةٍ

"The example of His light is that of a niche, in which there is a lamp; the lamp is in a glass." [101]

Ibn 'Abbās ﷺ interprets this section of the verse as referring to the heart of the Prophet ﷺ,

مَثَلُ نُورِهِ (فِي قَلْبِ نَبِيِّهِ) كَمِشْكَاةٍ فِيهَا مِصْبَاحٌ ـ الْمِصْبَاحُ فِي زُجَاجَةٍ

---

[101] Ibid.

"The example of His light [in the heart of His Prophet]
is that of a niche, in which there is a lamp;
the lamp is in a glass."

This section of the verse also mentions three key terms—
mishkāh (niche), *miṣbāḥ* (lamp) and *zujājah* (glass).

1. **Mishkāh**—Linguistically, this refers to a curved inflection
   in a wall or window, known as a niche. Before the invention
   of electric lighting, people would have niches in which
   candles could be placed in order to protect the delicate
   candlelight and cause it to bounce back and illuminate
   a wider area. These can easily be found in the corners of
   historic mosques built in Muslim lands. According to
   the interpretation of Ibn ʿAbbās ﷺ, the mishkāh (niche)
   in this verse refers to the blessed chest of the Prophet ﷺ.

2. **Miṣbāḥ**—This is the candle or lamp that is housed in the
   niche. This refers to Allah's ﷻ light and guidance.

3. **Zujājah**—This is glass or crystal in which the candle or
   lamp is kept for protection of the candlestick, wick, oil,
   and flame. The *zujājah* in this parable refers to the heart
   of the Prophet ﷺ, that protects and encloses the *miṣbāḥ*
   (lamp) of Allah's guidance, with this being housed in the
   mishkāh (niche) of the blessed chest of the Prophet ﷺ.

$$لَزُجَاجَةُ كَأَنَّهَا كَوْكَبٌ دُرِّيٌّ$$

"The glass looks like a brilliant star."[102]

The heart of the Prophet ﷺ is already the brightest star even before the candle is placed within it, shining with the light of the purity of his nature (*fiṭrah*).

$$يُوقَدُ مِن شَجَرَةٍ مُّبَارَكَةٍ زَيْتُونَةٍ$$

"It is lit from [the oil of] a blessed olive tree"[103]

The lamp obtains its oil from a blessed tree. There is a whole spectrum of interpretation as to what this tree is. One opinion is that it is the Noble Qur'an, which fits perfectly with the parable found in *Sūrah Ibrāhīm*, where one of the interpretations of a 'good tree' (*shajarah ṭayyibah*) is the Qur'an,

$$أَلَمْ تَرَ كَيْفَ ضَرَبَ اللَّهُ مَثَلًا كَلِمَةً طَيِّبَةً كَشَجَرَةٍ طَيِّبَةٍ$$
$$أَصْلُهَا ثَابِتٌ وَفَرْعُهَا فِي السَّمَاءِ$$

"Have you not seen how Allah has set forth a parable?
A good word is like a good tree whose root is firm
and whose branches are high in the sky."[104]

---

102 Ibid.

103 Ibid.

104 *Ibrāhīm*, 24.

According to the above-mentioned interpretation, the source of the oil that lights and sustains the flame is the Qur'an.

Another interpretation is that the blessed tree is the prophetic family tree of Ibrāhīm ﷺ. This is supported by the fact that the tree is described as '*zaytūnah*' (olive), which is a term that also comes in *Sūrah al-Tīn*,

وَالتِّينِ وَالزَّيْتُونِ

"By the fig and the olive [of Jerusalem]" [105]

According to one interpretation of this opening verse of *Sūrah al-Tīn*, the 'olive' (*zaytūn*) refers to Jerusalem; a city abundant with olives. As olive-laden Jerusalem is also a place where a considerable amount of Prophets ﷺ resided, the 'blessed olive tree' can thus refer to the blessed Abrahamic tree of Prophets ﷺ.

لَّا شَرْقِيَّةٍ وَلَا غَرْبِيَّةٍ

"Which is neither eastern, nor western." [106]

The next part of the Verse of Light informs us that the blessed tree is neither easterly nor westerly. If we interpret the blessed tree as the Qur'an, it will mean that the Qur'an

THE PARABLES OF THE QUR'AN

---

[105] *Al-Tīn*, 1.

[106] *Al-Nūr*, 35.

is not of this Earth, for it did not come from the east or west. Instead, it came directly from Allah ﷻ. If we interpret the blessed tree as Ibrāhīm ﷺ, it will refer to Ibrāhīm ﷺ not being Jewish nor Christian,

$$مَا كَانَ إِبْرَٰهِيمُ يَهُودِيًّا وَلَا نَصْرَانِيًّا وَلَٰكِن كَانَ حَنِيفًا مُّسْلِمًا وَمَا كَانَ مِنَ ٱلْمُشْرِكِينَ$$

"Ibrāhīm was neither a Jew nor a Christian; he submitted in all uprightness and was not a polytheist." [107]

The Verse of Light continues,

$$يَكَادُ زَيْتُهَا يُضِيءُ وَلَوْ لَمْ تَمْسَسْهُ نَارٌ$$

"Its oil is about to emit light even though the fire has not touched it." [108]

The oil is so pure, that it is emanating light itself even before it is set alight. This is in addition to the light of the lamp found within the glass. These are all,

$$نُّورٌ عَلَىٰ نُورٍ$$

"Light upon light!" [109]

---

[107] *Āl ʿImrān*, 67.

[108] *Al-Nūr*, 35.

[109] Ibid.

These are multiple layers of compound light. The Prophet ﷺ is from a blessed family; the entire genealogy of Ibrāhīm ﷺ is blessed, as the Qur'an informs us. In addition to this, his heart itself was pure from the start—he never worshipped false gods pre-prophethood, nor did he ever utter a lie. He was called *al-Ṣādiq* (the truthful) and *al-Amīn* (the trust-worthy) before being called a Prophet and Messenger. He was always a brilliant star. He was pure, his genealogy is pure, and the Qur'an that he was given is pure. This compounded light now becomes the ultimate source of guidance for all of humanity, for there is no path to reach Allah ﷻ other than the path of the Prophet ﷺ.

$$يَهْدِي اللَّهُ لِنُورِهِ مَن يَشَاءُ$$

"Allah guides whoever He wills to His light." [110]

This section of the verse proves that the whole metaphor is regarding the light of guidance.

$$وَيَضْرِبُ اللَّهُ الْأَمْثَالَ لِلنَّاسِ$$

"And Allah sets forth parables for humanity"

[110] Ibid.

وَاللَّهُ بِكُلِّ شَيْءٍ عَلِيمٌ

"For Allah has [perfect] knowledge of all things." [111]

This is where the Verse of Light ends, to be followed by a contrasting parable that discusses multiple layers of darkness.

May Allah ﷻ guide us to His light.

---

[111] Ibid.

لَعَلَّهُمْ يَتَفَكَّرُونَ

These are the parables we cite
for mankind so that they
can benefit and ponder.

AL-ḤASHR, 21.

SECTION TWO

Aphorisms

21

The Deeds of
the Disbeliever:
An Empty Illusion

Let us picture a person who opens a retirement fund. The fund gradually grows, steadily reaching $10,000, then $50,000, and after several decades half a million or more. As the owner of this fund approaches the age of retirement after years of hard work, he regularly checks his fund to ensure he has saved enough for his old age. However, imagine that one day he wakes up, and lo and behold, the account funds are zero. All of it is gone and untraceable, as if it never existed. May Allah ﷻ protect us from such a scenario.

The Qur'an presents parables of this sort in multiple places. These parables are primarily in relation to the disbeliever who does good deeds and thinks that he will attain benefit from them. But in reality, his deeds are not worthy of reward due to the abominable sin of disbelief and that the deeds were not done solely for Allah ﷻ. One such verse that addresses this scenario is found soon after the Verse of Light. Allah ﷻ first mentions that the righteous are those who obediently worship Allah ﷻ in the houses of Allah ﷻ. Allah ﷻ then presents the parable,

$$وَالَّذِينَ كَفَرُوا أَعْمَالُهُمْ كَسَرَابٍ بِقِيعَةٍ$$

"As for the disbelievers, their deeds are like
a mirage in a desert" [112]

The good deeds of the disbelievers have been likened to a mirage. A mirage is an optical illusion caused by atmospheric conditions, especially the appearance of a non-existent sheet of water in a desert caused by the refraction of light from the sky by heated air. This mirage that the disbelievers see is on flat desert land (*qīʿah*) that has no vegetation, as this is where the mirage is most powerful.

$$يَحْسَبُهُ الظَّمْآنُ مَاءً$$

"Which the thirsty perceive as water" [113]

---

[112] *Al-Nūr*, 39.

[113] Ibid.

The thirsty disbelievers think that the mirage is real water. However, once they reach there,

$$لَمْ يَجِدْهُ شَيْئًا$$

"They find it to be nothing."

There is no water to be found. Rather, instead of finding water,

$$وَوَجَدَ اللَّهَ عِندَهُ فَوَفَّاهُ حِسَابَهُ وَاللَّهُ سَرِيعُ الْحِسَابِ.$$

"Instead, they find Allah there [in the Hereafter, ready]
to settle their account. And Allah is swift in reckoning."

This is a description of the state of the disbeliever, who does good deeds mainly for fame and prestige. He dedicates buildings in his name, he goes to fancy fundraisers, and he makes large donations all for show. An innocent Muslim may think that this person lived a good life, as he donated to charity, supported the orphans, and did many other acts of kindness. Our response to this is that the one who does something for the sake of Allah ﷻ is not like the one who does something for the sake of his own ego. The one who acts for the sake of Allah ﷻ will be rewarded by Allah ﷻ, and the one who acts for other than Allah ﷻ will obviously not be rewarded by Allah ﷻ. Why should Allah ﷻ reward something not done for Him? Therefore, on the Day of Judgment, the disbeliever will come thinking that he has a large amount of deeds, but will find there that he has absolutely nothing.

In this regard, Allah ﷻ presents another parable in *Sūrah Ibrāhīm*,

مَّثَلُ الَّذِينَ كَفَرُوا بِرَبِّهِمْ ۖ أَعْمَالُهُمْ كَرَمَادٍ اشْتَدَّتْ بِهِ الرِّيحُ فِي يَوْمٍ عَاصِفٍ لَّا يَقْدِرُونَ مِمَّا كَسَبُوا عَلَىٰ شَيْءٍ

"The parable of the deeds of those who disbelieve in their Lord is that of ashes fiercely blown away by wind on a stormy day. They will gain nothing from what they have earned." [114]

When a fire is lit and ash is produced, you cannot collect the ash, as it will eventually be blown away by the winds. Allah ﷻ compares the good deeds of disbelievers to such ashes, as they are literally burning and dispersing their good deeds due to doing them for the wrong reasons.

A third parable on this topic is found in *Sūrah al-Furqān*,

وَقَدِمْنَا إِلَىٰ مَا عَمِلُوا مِنْ عَمَلٍ فَجَعَلْنَاهُ هَبَاءً مَّنثُورًا

"Then We will turn to whatever [good] deeds they did, reducing them to scattered dust." [115]

---

[114] *Ibrāhīm*, 18.

[115] *Al-Furqān*, 23.

All of the deeds that they thought that they had sent forward will become like dust that is scattered in the wind.

We thus have three powerful Qur'anic metaphors about good deeds done with corrupt intentions,

1. A mirage they think is water, but it is not really water.

2. Ashes they cannot collect.

3. Dust scattered in the wind.

In addition to these three verses, Allah ﷻ also says in *Sūrah al-Nūr*,

$$\text{أَوْ كَظُلُمَاتٍ فِي بَحْرٍ لُّجِّيٍّ}$$

"Or like the darkness in a deep sea" [116]

In interpreting this verse, one group of scholars says that it is another example of the deeds of the disbeliever. The translation would thus be,

"Or [the disbelievers' deeds are] like the darkness in a deep sea"

116 *Al-Nūr*, 40.

THE PARABLES OF THE QUR'AN

Another group of scholars say that it is an example of the heart of the disbeliever, contrasting with the Verse of Light that previously discussed the pure heart of the Prophet ﷺ.

> *"Or [the disbelievers' hearts are] like the*
> *darkness in a deep sea"*

Allah ﷻ is saying that their hearts are like the utter darkness of the lower levels of a deep ocean.

$$يَغْشَىٰهُ مَوْجٌ مِّن فَوْقِهِۦ مَوْجٌ مِّن فَوْقِهِۦ سَحَابٌ ۚ ظُلُمَٰتٌ بَعْضُهَا فَوْقَ بَعْضٍ$$

> *"Covered by waves upon waves, topped by [dark] clouds.*
> *Darkness upon darkness!"* [117]

There is a dark ocean, covered by multiple layers of crashing waves in the dark night, upon which are dark clouds, creating layers of darkness. This is a terrible scene and the complete opposite to the 'light upon light' (*nūr 'alā nūr*) mentioned in the Verse of Light. Personally, this reminds me of one occasion when I went scuba diving at night and a thunderstorm suddenly began in the middle of the ocean. It was one of the most terrifying experiences of my life. This powerful verse came to mind as the waves were crashing upon me and we awaited the return of the boat to save us by Allah's ﷻ grace.

---

[117] Ibid.

It is also very interesting that Allah ﷻ mentions such an oceanic example to the desert dwellers of Arabia, who had no experience of seafaring in the ocean. Yet, Allah ﷻ describes this scene in vivid detail because the darkness of the ocean is unique and terrifying. Scholars say that the ocean represents the depths of the darkness of the heart of the disbeliever, the waves represent his own inner doubts, and the clouds represent the outer influences that are harming him, such as his evil friends and society. Everything within and around him is dark. It is so dark that if he were to put his hand out, he would not be able to see it, or he would see it with great difficulty.

إِذَا أَخْرَجَ يَدَهُ لَمْ يَكَدْ يَرَاهَا وَمَن لَّمْ يَجْعَلِ اللَّهُ لَهُ نُورًا فَمَا لَهُ مِن نُّورٍ

"If one stretches out their hand, they can hardly see it.
And whoever Allah does not bless with light
will have no light!" [118]

The closing part of the verse informs us that if Allah ﷻ does not give you the light of guidance via His Book and Prophets ﷺ, where will you obtain light from? If you have chosen to remain in the darkness of your heart, desires, doubt, and company you have chosen, then Allah ﷻ is not going to give to you that light because you do not deserve it.

118 Ibid.

This is a key point—anybody who wishes for guidance will find it, and the one who does not want guidance will be left to wander astray.

We ask Allah ﷻ to bless us with His light and to save us all from darkness.

22

The Futile and Vain Proofs
of the Disbelievers

I n this chapter, we will be exploring two Qur'anic parables that condemn the association of partners with Allah ﷻ (*shirk*). The first is found in verse 41 of *Sūrah al-'Ankabūt*,

مَثَلُ الَّذِينَ اتَّخَذُوا مِن دُونِ اللَّهِ أَوْلِيَاءَ كَمَثَلِ الْعَنكَبُوتِ اتَّخَذَتْ بَيْتًا ۖ
وَإِنَّ أَوْهَنَ الْبُيُوتِ لَبَيْتُ الْعَنكَبُوتِ ۚ لَوْ كَانُوا يَعْلَمُونَ

"The parable of those who take protectors other than Allah is that of a spider spinning a shelter. And the flimsiest of all shelters is certainly that of a spider, if only they knew." [119]

This profound parable gives a strong message, and the more we analyse it from a scientific perspective the more powerful

---

[119] *Al-'Ankabūt*, 41.

it becomes. Scientists tell us that the spider's web is made from a particular type of protein that is one of the strongest materials in terms of elasticity and tensile strength. However, since it is super thin, it is easy for larger creatures or the wind to break it. Yet, if a large creature such as a human was able to produce something of its like, it would be almost ten times stronger than steel. For this reason, spiderwebs are miraculous structures that are still under study, with some laboratories attempting to create an imitation of them. This is because they are movable, thin yet strong, and very malleable. If we could produce such webs ourselves, we would be able to construct better-fortified buildings and use them for various useful purposes. Having said that, despite many efforts, we still do not have that technology, as Allah ﷻ has naturally gifted the spider with that know-how.

In the parable, Allah ﷻ informs us that those who think that other gods apart from Him can protect them are victims of fanciful thinking, for only He is our Lord and Protector. The example of such fanciful thinkers is like a spider that creates a web as a shelter, despite it being the weakest and flimsiest of all shelters. Interestingly, the parable here calls the spiderweb the weakest of shelters, despite the truth being that the spiderweb is not a shelter at all. A shelter or home is used for protection against the elements and enemies, but the spider's web does not protect against any of these things. Thus, it cannot be a shelter or a home. Rather, the web's true purpose is as a trap meant to catch bugs and insects. This is powerful, as back at the time of revelation who would have known that the spider's web is not even a shelter? Thus, when Allah ﷻ says that it is the weakest of shelters, this is because it is not actually meant as a shelter, and will not provide any protection. This is how Allah ﷻ shows how weak the example is of the one who associates partners with Him.

The second parable is found in verse 31 of *Sūrah al-Ḥajj*. Allah ﷻ says,

حُنَفَاءَ لِلَّهِ غَيْرَ مُشْرِكِينَ بِهِ ۚ وَمَن يُشْرِكْ بِاللَّهِ فَكَأَنَّمَا خَرَّ مِنَ السَّمَاءِ فَتَخْطَفُهُ الطَّيْرُ أَوْ تَهْوِي بِهِ الرِّيحُ فِي مَكَانٍ سَحِيقٍ

"Be upright [in devotion] to Allah, associating none with Him [in worship]. For whoever associates [others] with Allah is like someone who has fallen from the sky and is either snatched away by birds or swept by the wind to a remote place." [120]

This is a powerful verse that talks about the reality of *shirk*. Those who worship other than Allah ﷻ are like people falling from the skies, who are then snatched away by vultures and birds or thrown by heavy winds to a faraway place. This compliments other Qur'anic parables, such as the parable of the good tree that talks about the rising of the proclamation of His oneness (*tawḥīd*), which is the opposite of *shirk*. In this parable, Allah ﷻ is comparing *tawḥīd* to the vastness of the sky, and how testifying to *lā ilāha illa Allāh* will

THE PARABLES OF THE QUR'AN

---

120 *Al-Ḥajj*, 31.

take you upwards in the sky. *Tawḥīd* is vast and elevating, whilst *shirk* will cause you to come crashing down. Just as the person falling from a mountain or plane cannot be saved without a parachute or aid, you cannot save yourself if you commit *shirk*, and no one will aid you in any way. The one who commits *shirk* is headed to his own destruction, falling and crashing into the fires of *Jahannam*.

As for the birds and winds, Ibn al-Qayyim ﷺ and others say that the birds represent the different devils, and the wind represents your desires. The devils will snatch bits and pieces of you, each grabbing a portion of your heart until you have nothing left, or you allow your own desires to cause you to go astray. Such a person did not attain salvation by taking hold of the stable rope of Allah ﷻ, so he will continue falling to his destruction.

May Allah ﷻ save us from such a terrible falling.

23

The Eminent Rank of
Knowledge and
its Possessors

In *Sūrah al-Zumar*, we find a rhetorical question within one of the most commonly quoted verses of the Noble Qur'an. Allah ﷺ says,

قُلْ هَلْ يَسْتَوِي الَّذِينَ يَعْلَمُونَ وَالَّذِينَ لَا يَعْلَمُونَ

*"Say, [O Prophet,] 'Are those who know equal
to those who do not know?'"* [121]

In this verse, Allah ﷺ emphasises the superiority of the person who possesses knowledge in comparison to one who does not by using a rhetorical question. This theme of demonstrating the superiority and blessings of knowledge is repeated in the Qur'an. In reality, the Qur'an itself was revealed to spread

---

[121] *Al-Zumar*, 9.

knowledge and educate, as is understood from the very first revelation being the command 'Read!' It is a Blessed Book that was sent to impart the primary knowledge that informs us of the purpose of our lives—the servitude of Allah ﷻ. Therefore, knowledge leads us to recognise that there is no true deity except Allah ﷻ, and the one who rejects this is devoid of true knowledge. In another verse, Allah ﷻ praises knowledge and the people of knowledge,

يَرْفَعِ اللَّهُ الَّذِينَ آمَنُوا مِنكُمْ وَالَّذِينَ أُوتُوا الْعِلْمَ دَرَجَاتٍ

"Allah will elevate those of you who are faithful, and [raise] those gifted with knowledge in rank." [122]

Allah ﷻ raises the ranks of people purely through virtue of knowledge.

From the verse of *Sūrah Āl 'Imrān*, we also understand that Allah ﷻ places the people of knowledge in a similar category to the angels by mentioning them both together.

شَهِدَ اللَّهُ أَنَّهُ لاَ إِلَهَ إِلاَّ هُوَ وَالْمَلاَئِكَةُ وَأُوْلُواْ الْعِلْمِ قَآئِمَاً بِالْقِسْطِ

"Allah [Himself] is a Witness that there is no god [worthy of worship] except Him—and so are the angels and people of knowledge. He is the Maintainer of justice." [123]

[122] *Al-Mujādilah*, 11.

[123] *Āl 'Imrān*, 19.

Ibn al-Qayyim says that this is the highest praise that Allah has bestowed upon the people of knowledge. Allah ﷻ, the angels, and the people of knowledge all testify to His Oneness in unison.

Knowledge was also a primary cause of our Prophet ﷺ being honoured with his lofty status, in addition to his perfect character and divine designation as the best of mankind. Allah ﷻ says in the Qur'an,

$$وَأَنزَلَ ٱللَّهُ عَلَيْكَ ٱلْكِتَٰبَ وَٱلْحِكْمَةَ وَعَلَّمَكَ مَا لَمْ تَكُن تَعْلَمُ ۚ وَكَانَ فَضْلُ ٱللَّهِ عَلَيْكَ عَظِيمًا$$

"Allah has revealed to you the Book and wisdom and taught you what you never knew. Great [indeed] is Allah's favour upon you!" [124]

Allah ﷻ also says,

$$وَوَجَدَكَ ضَآلًّا فَهَدَىٰ$$

"Did He not find you unguided then guided you?" [125]

$$وَكَذَٰلِكَ أَوْحَيْنَآ إِلَيْكَ رُوحًا مِّنْ أَمْرِنَا ۚ مَا كُنتَ تَدْرِى مَا ٱلْكِتَٰبُ وَلَا ٱلْإِيمَٰنُ وَلَٰكِن جَعَلْنَٰهُ نُورًا نَّهْدِى بِهِۦ مَن نَّشَآءُ مِنْ عِبَادِنَا ۚ$$

124 *Al-Nisā'*, 113.

125 *Al-Ḍuḥā*, 7.

"And so We have sent to you [O Prophet] a revelation by Our command. You did not know of [this] Book and faith [before]. But We have made it a light, by which We guide whoever We will of Our servants." [126]

These verses all indicate that the rank of our Prophet ﷺ was raised through knowledge. In relation to the other Prophets of Allah ﷻ, their status was also raised through knowledge (*'ilm*) and wisdom (*ḥikmah*). For example, Allah says that we gave Dāwūd ﷺ knowledge and wisdom. He also says that We gave Sulaymān ﷺ understanding (*fahm*),

$$فَفَهَّمْنَاهَا سُلَيْمَانَ$$

"And We gave understanding of it [the case] to Sulaymān." [127]

The family of Ibrāhīm ﷺ was also blessed with wisdom; all the Prophets of Allah ﷺ were given wisdom. Of all these verses that reference knowledge, there is one encompassing verse that we should all memorise and understand,

$$إِنَّمَا يَخْشَى اللَّهَ مِنْ عِبَادِهِ الْعُلَمَاءُ$$

"It is those of His servants who have knowledge who stand in true awe of Allah." [128]

---

126 *Al-Shūrā*, 52.

127 *Al-Anbiyāʾ*, 79.

128 *Fāṭir*, 28.

Upon reading this verse, a person who does not have extensive knowledge may start to think that they cannot achieve true fear and consciousness of Allah (*khashyah*). The response to this is that the 'knowledge' mentioned in this verse is not the knowledge held by a jurist, exegete, or Mufti, but it is the widely accessible knowledge of Allah's ﷻ recognition and worship. This is the simple and primary type of knowledge being lauded. Knowledge of jurisprudence (*fiqh*), exegesis (*tafsīr*), principles (*uṣūl*), and other Islamic sciences are important, yet still secondary. The evidence for this is found at the start of the very verse of *Sūrah al-Zumar* that is currently under discussion. Describing the true people of knowledge, Allah ﷻ says,

أَمَّنْ هُوَ قَٰنِتٌ ءَانَآءَ ٱلَّيْلِ سَاجِدًا وَقَآئِمًا يَحْذَرُ ٱلْءَاخِرَةَ وَيَرْجُواْ رَحْمَةَ رَبِّهِۦ قُلْ هَلْ يَسْتَوِى ٱلَّذِينَ يَعْلَمُونَ وَٱلَّذِينَ لَا يَعْلَمُونَ إِنَّمَا يَتَذَكَّرُ أُوْلُواْ ٱلْأَلْبَٰبِ

"[Are they better] or those who worship [their Lord] devoutly in the hours of the night, prostrating and standing, fearing the Hereafter, and hoping for the mercy of their Lord? Say, [O Prophet,] 'Are those who know equal to those who do not know?'"

Allah ﷻ presents the example of the one fervently offering the nightly vigil (*tahajjud*). Immediately after this, Allah then makes the statement regarding knowledge, indicating that the worship of Allah ﷻ such as *tahajjud* is the knowledge being referred to. This transpires when a person takes their studied knowledge and then translates it into action.

Such a person is the one with true understanding. On the other hand, just memorising books, facts, and discussions is not praiseworthy itself unless accompanied by action. In fact, Allah ﷻ criticises superficial knowledge that does not lead to action. Allah ﷻ says:

يَعْلَمُونَ ظَاهِرًا مِّنَ الْحَيَاةِ الدُّنْيَا وَهُمْ عَنِ الْآخِرَةِ هُمْ غَافِلُونَ

"They [only] know the worldly affairs of this life, but are [totally] oblivious to the Hereafter." [129]

They have advanced to such a degree that they know how to travel to the moon and back, they understand the nature of the atom and sub-atomic particles, they know of all the mechanisms of this world, but they are still heedlessly oblivious of the Hereafter. All of that knowledge is wasted. It matters not how many Nobel Prizes a person wins for advancements in the sciences if they cannot save their own soul. This is not to say secular knowledge is useless, but we need to strike a balance. The best of people strive to hold both knowledge of Allah ﷻ and knowledge of the world, using both of these to recognise their Creator, increase in action, and rise in rank.

---

[129] *Al-Rūm*, 7.

After understanding this, let us now make an intention to associate ourselves with knowledge and learn the basics of the religion. Let us learn the correct enunciation and brief meaning of the Qur'an that we are reciting, the necessary basics of jurisprudence, and the correct methods of worshipping Allah ﷻ. These are the very basics we should all aim for. Not every person will become a scholar (*ālim*), nor is that even necessary. But no person should remain as an ignoramus (*jāhil*). Every person can learn what they can according to their own capacity, even if that be through attending local study circles and lectures. If we do so, remember the promise of Allah ﷻ,

$$ يَرْفَعِ اللَّهُ الَّذِينَ آمَنُوا مِنكُمْ وَالَّذِينَ أُوتُوا الْعِلْمَ دَرَجَاتٍ $$

"Allah will elevate those of you who are faithful, and [raise] those gifted with knowledge in rank." [130]

May Allah ﷻ make us from amongst those people.

---

[130] *Al-Mujādilah*, 11.

24

The Praiseworthy Qualities of the Companions

We find in the final verse of *Sūrah al-Fatḥ* (The Chapter of the Conquest) the only Qur'anic parable about the Companions of the Messenger ﷺ (*ṣaḥābah*). This *sūrah* was revealed after the Treaty of Hudaybiyyah when the mood of the Companions ﷺ was low, as they thought that they had been outwit by the Quraysh. Allah ﷻ then revealed that they had actually been victorious,

إِنَّا فَتَحْنَا لَكَ فَتْحًا مُّبِينًا

"Indeed, We have granted you a clear triumph [O Prophet]" [131]

---

[131] *Al-Fatḥ*, 1.

Due to this glad tiding, Our Prophet ﷺ said that this *surah* is more beloved to him than the whole world and all that it contains. As mentioned, the final verse of the *surah* is about the Companions ﷺ. There is a subtle indication in this that one of the victories and conquests that Allah ﷻ had given the Prophet ﷺ was his Companions ﷺ, for they played a vital role in spreading Islam and are one of the reasons why this religion is blessed.

The final verse begins with the famous Qur'anic phrase that is one of the few places where our Prophet ﷺ is mentioned by name,

مُحَمَّدٌ رَّسُولُ اللَّهِ

"Muhammad is the Messenger of Allah." [132]

This phrase that constitutes a part of our testimony of faith appears only here in the Qur'an.

مُحَمَّدٌ رَّسُولُ اللَّهِ ۚ وَالَّذِينَ مَعَهُۥٓ أَشِدَّآءُ عَلَى الْكُفَّارِ رُحَمَآءُ بَيْنَهُمْ ۖ تَرَىٰهُمْ رُكَّعًا سُجَّدًا يَبْتَغُونَ فَضْلًا مِّنَ اللَّهِ وَرِضْوَٰنًا ۖ سِيمَاهُمْ فِي وُجُوهِهِم مِّنْ أَثَرِ السُّجُودِ ۚ ذَٰلِكَ مَثَلُهُمْ فِي التَّوْرَىٰةِ ۚ وَمَثَلُهُمْ فِي الْإِنجِيلِ كَزَرْعٍ أَخْرَجَ شَطْئَهُۥ فَآزَرَهُۥ فَاسْتَغْلَظَ فَاسْتَوَىٰ عَلَىٰ سُوقِهِۦ يُعْجِبُ الزُّرَّاعَ لِيَغِيظَ بِهِمُ الْكُفَّارَ ۗ وَعَدَ اللَّهُ الَّذِينَ ءَامَنُوا وَعَمِلُوا الصَّٰلِحَٰتِ مِنْهُم مَّغْفِرَةً وَأَجْرًا عَظِيمًا

175

"Muhammad is the Messenger of Allah. And those with him are firm with the disbelievers and compassionate with one another. You see them bowing and prostrating [in prayer], seeking Allah's bounty and pleasure. The sign [of brightness can be seen] on their faces from the trace of prostrating [in prayer]. This is their description in the Torah. And their parable in the Gospel is that of a seed that sprouts its [tiny] branches, making it strong. Then it becomes thick, standing firmly on its stem, to the delight of the planters—in this way Allah makes the believers a source of dismay for the disbelievers. To those of them who believe and do good, Allah has promised forgiveness and a great reward." [133]

In this verse, the Companions ﷺ are described as 'firm with the disbelievers and compassionate with one another'. We see this characteristic of the Companions ﷺ in their harshness against enemies such as Abū Jahl, Abū Lahab, and 'Utbah ibn Rabī'ah; whilst being merciful and tender amongst themselves. You will also observe that they were constantly worshipping Allah ﷺ with love and hope, seeking Allah's ﷺ pleasure, unlimited blessings, forgiveness, mercy, and His paradise. Due to this abundant worship, there are marks of prostration on their faces.

There are a number of interpretations as to what the marks of prostration are. One interpretation is that it is a physical

---

[133] Ibid.

mark found upon the forehead, such as the naturally occurring mark that can be made when a person prostrates on gravel or sand for a long period of time. Nonetheless, we do not make attempts to rub our heads onto the floor and carpet to attain such a mark, as it is from Allah ﷻ.

A second valid interpretation is that you will find the effects of prostration on their faces, referring to the light of faith—their demeanour, respect, and their overall interactions. Their faith will spiritually manifest on their faces.

A third valid interpretation is that on the Day of Judgment you will find their faces shining bright, as our Prophet ﷺ said, "My nation will come with their faces and hands shining bright."

Allah ﷻ then says that this is how they are described in the Torah (*Tawrāh*) and the Gospel (*Injīl*). Amazingly, Allah ﷻ has predictively praised the Companions ﷺ using parables in the verses revealed to Mūsā ﷺ and 'Īsā ﷺ, informing them that a final Prophet will come who will have praiseworthy Companions ﷺ. For example, if you open Mark:24 from the New Testament, you may find the parable where 'Īsā ﷺ gives his disciples an example about a seed that is planted and grows stronger.

Though this parable in the New Testament may not be correctly worded due to biblical corruption, the Qur'an informs us of its existence in the original,

وَمَثَلُهُمْ فِى ٱلْإِنجِيلِ كَزَرْعٍ أَخْرَجَ شَطْـَٔهُۥ فَـَٔازَرَهُۥ فَٱسْتَغْلَظَ فَٱسْتَوَىٰ عَلَىٰ سُوقِهِۦ يُعْجِبُ ٱلزُّرَّاعَ لِيَغِيظَ بِهِمُ ٱلْكُفَّارَ

"And their parable in the Gospel is that of a seed that sprouts its [tiny] branches, making it strong. Then it becomes thick, standing firmly on its stem, to the delight of the planters —in this way Allah makes the believers a source of dismay for the disbelievers."

An originally small seed sprouts into tiny branches or leaves such as those found on a beanstalk or pea pod, eventually growing firmer and stronger. This amazes and gladdens those who planted it, just as the Companions ﷺ loved to see their belief growing and becoming stronger. As for the disbelievers, they become more irritated by this growth. However, this matters not as,

وَعَدَ ٱللَّهُ ٱلَّذِينَ آمَنُوا وَعَمِلُوا ٱلصَّالِحَاتِ مِنْهُم مَّغْفِرَةً وَأَجْرًا عَظِيمًا

"To those of them who believe and do good, Allah has promised forgiveness and a great reward."

This complete parable describes how the Companions ﷺ were originally few and weak, such that they were mercilessly persecuted and forced to hide their Islam. At that

stage, they were like the good seed that is hidden, but will gradually struggle and grow until it reaches perfection. This is exactly how Islam began: with gradual growth, eventually becoming a beautiful tree—a concept reinforced by other Qur'anic parables that equate a good tree with faith. This tree grew under the supervision of the Companions ﷺ.

The famous Successor (*tābi'ī*) Ḥasan al-Baṣrī ﷺ presented an interesting symbolic exegesis (*tafsīr ishārī*) of this verse. He posited that each of the four phrases in this parable represents the eras of the four rightly guided successors in which Islam continued to grow. The seed was the Prophet ﷺ, and the first leaf that came from it was Abū Bakr al-Ṣiddīq ﷺ. It grew firmer and stronger with 'Umar ibn al-Khaṭṭāb ﷺ, larger and thicker with 'Uthmān ibn 'Affān ﷺ, and then ended standing firmly on its stem with 'Alī ibn Abī Ṭālib ﷺ. This exegesis again points to the praise of the Companions ﷺ, as the roots of this religion go back to them and their sacrifices to make the tree of Islam strong.

In the time of Imam Mālik ﷺ, a man from an unorthodox group came to the Imam and started speaking virulently about the Companions ﷺ. Imam Mālik ﷺ then quoted this verse and explained that anybody who hates the Companions ﷺ is agreeing with the disbelievers. It is not possible that a pure heart will hold anything evil against the Companions ﷺ, as Allah ﷻ has praised them in over 15 verses in the Qur'an. This is why we respect them, love them, and invoke mercy upon them when taking their noble names.

رَضِىَ اللهُ عَنْهُمْ وَ رَضُوْا عَنْه

*"Allah is pleased with them and
they are pleased with Him."* [134]

Our Prophet ﷺ commanded us not to speak ill of his
Companions ﷺ, for if one of us were to do good that
amounts to the size of the mountain of Uḥud, it would still
not be equal to a handful of what they have done. The sacrifices and efforts that they made when Islam and Muslims
were weak and persecuted can never be compared to what
we are doing today, with Islam already a major civilisation
having approximately a billion members around the world.
This is why the status of the Companions ﷺ is so exalted.

May Allah ﷻ have mercy on all of the Companions ﷺ.

134 *Bayyinah*, 8.

25

The Danger of Abstract Knowledge
Without Sincere Belief and Action

In *Sūrah al-Jumuʿah*, Allah ﷻ presents a warning to us in one of the harshest and bluntest Qur'anic parables. The stern wording of this parable is such that it makes our hearts cringe and convinces us that we do not want to be of the evil ones whom this parable discusses. Allah ﷻ says,

مَثَلُ الَّذِينَ حُمِّلُوا التَّوْرَاةَ ثُمَّ لَمْ يَحْمِلُوهَا كَمَثَلِ الْحِمَارِ يَحْمِلُ أَسْفَارًا ۚ بِئْسَ مَثَلُ الْقَوْمِ الَّذِينَ كَذَّبُوا بِآيَاتِ اللَّهِ

"The example of those who were entrusted with [observing] the Torah but failed to do so, is that of a donkey carrying books. How evil is the example of those who reject Allah's signs! For Allah does not guide the wrongdoing people." [135]

---

[135] *Al-Jumuʿah*, 5.

This parable is about the Children of Israel, a people who Allah ﷻ blessed immensely as His chosen people. Allah ﷻ says,

يَٰبَنِىٓ إِسْرَٰٓءِيلَ ٱذْكُرُواْ نِعْمَتِىَ ٱلَّتِىٓ أَنْعَمْتُ عَلَيْكُمْ وَأَنِّى فَضَّلْتُكُمْ عَلَى ٱلْعَٰلَمِينَ

"O Children of Israel! Remember [all] the favours
I granted you and how I honoured you above the others." [136]

Allah ﷻ also says,

وَآتَاكُم مَّا لَمْ يُؤْتِ أَحَدًا مِّنَ الْعَالَمِينَ

"And [Allah] gave you what He had never
given anyone in the world." [137]

The Children of Israel are mentioned over 70 times in the Qur'an, thus forming a primary motif of the divine scripture. This is as their civilisation, faith, theology, laws, rituals, customs, and habits closely correspond to ours—from a historical perspective—more than any other people. Even today, the orthodox Jews to an extent resemble us in general theology, rituals, laws, and habitual customs, such as in the manner of eating and dressing. By mentioning them copiously in the Qur'an, Allah ﷻ is urging us to reflect on their stories in order to extract the good, as well as to learn from their errors, which will help us to avoid falling prey

---

[136] *Al-Baqarah*, 47.

[137] *Al-Mā'idah*, 20.

to the same disobedience and mistakes they made. Despite being the blessed chosen people, they abused their blessings, did not fulfil their responsibilities, and were ungrateful to Allah ﷻ. It is due to this diabolical behaviour that they were criticised, not because of their ancestry or identity, as this would not be within the parameters of Islamic justice. There is no discrimination or racism in Islam. This is why every verse in the Qur'an that criticises them only does so after mentioning their evil deeds, such as,

$$
\text{فَبِمَا نَقْضِهِم مِّيثَـٰقَهُمْ لَعَنَّـٰهُمْ وَجَعَلْنَا قُلُوبَهُمْ قَـٰسِيَةً ۖ يُحَرِّفُونَ ٱلْكَلِمَ عَن مَّوَاضِعِهِۦ ۙ وَنَسُوا۟ حَظًّا مِّمَّا ذُكِّرُوا۟ بِهِۦ}
$$

"But for breaking their covenant We condemned them and hardened their hearts. They distorted the words of the Scripture and neglected a portion of what they had been commanded to uphold." [138]

$$
\text{وَتَرَىٰ كَثِيرًا مِّنْهُمْ يُسَـٰرِعُونَ فِى ٱلْإِثْمِ وَٱلْعُدْوَٰنِ وَأَكْلِهِمُ ٱلسُّحْتَ ۚ لَبِئْسَ مَا كَانُوا۟ يَعْمَلُونَ}
$$

"You see many of them racing towards sin, transgression, and consumption of forbidden gain. Evil indeed are their actions!" [139]

THE PARABLES OF THE QUR'AN

---

138 *Al-Mā'idah*, 13.

139 *Al-Mā'idah*, 62.

وَأَخْذِهِمُ ٱلرِّبَوٰاْ وَقَدْ نُهُواْ عَنْهُ وَأَكْلِهِمْ أَمْوَٰلَ ٱلنَّاسِ بِٱلْبَٰطِلِ

"Taking interest despite its prohibition,
and consuming people's wealth unjustly." [140]

On the topic of interest, Allah ﷻ forbade it in previous scriptures too. For example, a verse in Deuteronomy can still be found to this effect. Despite knowing this, the Children of Israel in European banking history are noted to have dealt and profited from interest-fuelled business and transactions.

Allah ﷻ also conferred upon the Children of Israel the honour of holding a line of Prophets. From Yaʿqūb ﷺ all the way to ʿĪsā ﷺ, they were sent continuous Prophets in every generation. When one Prophet would pass away, another Prophet would be sent immediately in his place. No other civilisation was given the honour of having such a chain of Prophets protecting and guiding them. However, they were not appreciative of this, and shockingly attempted to kill some of their own prophets,

فَبِمَا نَقْضِهِم مِّيثَٰقَهُمْ وَكُفْرِهِم بِـَٔايَٰتِ ٱللَّهِ وَقَتْلِهِمُ ٱلْأَنۢبِيَآءَ بِغَيْرِ حَقٍّ وَقَوْلِهِمْ
قُلُوبُنَا غُلْفٌ ۚ بَلْ طَبَعَ ٱللَّهُ عَلَيْهَا بِكُفْرِهِمْ فَلَا يُؤْمِنُونَ إِلَّا قَلِيلًا

"[They were condemned] for breaking their covenant,
rejecting Allah's signs, killing the prophets unjustly,
and for saying, 'Our hearts are unreceptive!'"

---

[140] *Al-Nisāʾ*, 161.

This culminated in their despicable treatment of the great and noble Messenger ʿĪsā ☙. After this, Allah ☙ decided to remove His blessing from them, and their status was lifted away due to their own misdeeds.

Their arrogant disobedience is also demonstrated in the incident of our mother Ṣafiyyah ☙, who was brought up in a Jewish household. When she was a young girl, her father and uncle visited the Prophet ☙ to verify what was going on in Madinah. When they learnt of the call of the Prophet ☙, they returned home distressed and distraught. This was to the extent that they began ignoring her, even though they usually loved playing with her. She heard her father ask her uncle if he (our Prophet ☙) was the one, to which he replied in the affirmative. Her father then asked her uncle as to what course of action they should take, to which her uncle replied that he will hate our Prophet ☙ and oppose him until death. Allah ☙ revealed these types of verses due to such individuals who knew the truth and shunned it. Allah ☙ says,

يَعْرِفُونَهُۥ كَمَا يَعْرِفُونَ أَبْنَآءَهُمُ ٱلَّذِينَ ءَاتَيْنَٰهُمُ ٱلْكِتَٰبَ يَعْرِفُونَهُۥ كَمَا يَعْرِفُونَ أَبْنَآءَهُمْ ۖ وَإِنَّ فَرِيقًا مِّنْهُمْ لَيَكْتُمُونَ ٱلْحَقَّ وَهُمْ يَعْلَمُونَ

"Those We have given the Scripture recognise this [Prophet] as they recognise their own children. Yet a group of them hides the truth knowingly." [141]

---

[141] *Al-Baqarah*, 46.

It is due to arrogance and disobedience of this type that Allah ﷻ says,

مَثَلُ الَّذِينَ حُمِّلُوا التَّوْرَاةَ ثُمَّ لَمْ يَحْمِلُوهَا كَمَثَلِ الْحِمَارِ يَحْمِلُ أَسْفَارًا بِئْسَ مَثَلُ الْقَوْمِ الَّذِينَ كَذَّبُوا بِآيَاتِ اللَّهِ

"The example of those who were entrusted with [observing] the Torah but failed to do so, is that of a donkey carrying books. How evil is the example of those who reject Allah's signs! For Allah does not guide the wrongdoing people."

Those who possessed knowledge and turned away from the truth have been likened to donkeys, which are a universal object of ridicule. Allah ﷻ says in the Qur'an,

إِنَّ أَنْكَرَ الْأَصْوَاتِ لَصَوْتُ الْحَمِيرِ

"The ugliest of all voices is certainly the braying of donkeys." [142]

They have been likened to a donkey carrying books; the load of books is all on its back, but they hold no value for the donkey, as it cannot benefit from them. Similarly, what use is abundant knowledge for humankind if it will not be practised on and used to accept truth?

---

[142] *Luqmān*, 19.

This parable is similar to the parable of the dog, that also describes the one who knew the truth but stubbornly refused to accept it,

كَمَثَلِ ٱلْكَلْبِ إِن تَحْمِلْ عَلَيْهِ يَلْهَثْ أَوْ تَتْرُكْهُ يَلْهَث

"His example is that of a dog: if you chase it away, it pants, and if you leave it, it [still] pants." [143]

It is important to bear in mind that these parables apply to individuals who arrogantly reject the truth despite clearly knowing it. As for those who know the truth but do not act upon it due to weakness, the scholars say that these exact examples would not apply to them. However, they should still fear reproach due to the delicate nature of this issue.

It is also very interesting that following the parable of the donkey, Allah ﷻ mentions the Friday address (*khuṭbah*),

يَٰٓأَيُّهَا ٱلَّذِينَ ءَامَنُوٓاْ إِذَا نُودِيَ لِلصَّلَوٰةِ مِن يَوْمِ ٱلْجُمُعَةِ فَٱسْعَوْاْ إِلَىٰ ذِكْرِ ٱللَّهِ وَذَرُواْ ٱلْبَيْعَ ۚ ذَٰلِكُمْ خَيْرٌ لَّكُمْ إِن كُنتُمْ تَعْلَمُونَ

"O believers! When the call to prayer is made on Friday, then proceed [diligently] to the remembrance of Allah [the khuṭbah] and leave of [your] business. That is best for you, if only you knew." [144]

THE PARABLES OF THE QUR'AN

---

[143] *Al-A'rāf*, 176.

[144] *Al-Jumu'ah*, 9.

Allah ﷻ mentions the *khuṭbah* right after warning people against rejecting despite knowing, as in every *khuṭbah* you are reminded of the basic fundamentals and essentials of Islam. When we hear these pieces of advice, we must try our best to implement them so that not even a portion of this terrifying parable applies to us. Even if we fail or struggle in implementation, never let this make you walk the precipitous slope of justifying evil and rejecting truth. Keep on striving and ask for Allah's ﷻ forgiveness.

We seek Allah's ﷻ refuge from ever being like the dog or donkey, and we ask Allah ﷻ to be of His righteous and pious worshippers.

26

Aphorisms Concerning Preaching and Practising One's Faith

Our discourse thus far has been focused on Qur'anic parables. But now we will shift our focus to the theme of aphorisms. To recap, a Qur'anic aphorism is a phrase that has become symbolic in Arab linguistic culture and is viewed as a revered statement of utmost wisdom—such that it will have found its way into becoming part of the vernacular of societies and civilisations.

In this chapter, we will highlight a few Qur'anic aphorisms.

In verse 44 of *Sūrah al-Baqarah*, Allah ﷻ makes a powerful statement containing a rhetorical question. Addressing the Children of Israel, Allah ﷻ says,

اَتَأْمُرُونَ النَّاسَ بِالْبِرِّ وَتَنْسَوْنَ اَنْفُسَكُمْ

"Do you preach righteousness and fail to practice it
yourselves, although you read the Scripture?
Do you not understand?" [145]

This phrase has become commonly used in the Arabic language, and is seen as an eloquent expression. It is an expression that showcases the hypocrisy of those individuals that concentrate on the faults of others whilst ignoring and neglecting their own faults. This is done by utilising a rhetorical question—originally aimed at the Children of Israel—that is a form of rebuke and highlights the nonsensical nature of such behaviour. If we look towards the example of the noble Prophets ﷺ, we find that their actions would always speak louder than their words. They were perfect role models for mankind in terms of both their behaviour and speech. Since he is at the pinnacle of sublime prophetic character, our Prophet ﷺ holds a distinguished platform,

وَإِنَّكَ لَعَلَى خُلُقٍ عَظِيمٍ

"And you are truly [a man] of
outstanding character." [146]

---

[145] *Al-Baqarah*, 44.

[146] *Al-Qalam*, 4.

Allah ﷻ also says,

$$\text{لَقَدْ كَانَ لَكُمْ فِيْ رَسُوْلِ اللهِ أُسْوَةٌ حَسَنَةٌ}$$

"Indeed, in the Messenger of Allah you have an excellent
example for whoever has hope in Allah and the Last Day,
and remembers Allah often." [147]

The Prophets of Allah ﷺ and those who wish to follow their
path must ensure that their actions speak louder than their
words. Allah criticizes these people from the Children of
Israel who did the exact opposite: constantly commanding
and preaching to others whilst not practising themselves.
Allah ﷻ also criticises such behaviour in another verse,

$$\text{يَآ أَيُّهَا الَّذِيْنَ اٰمَنُوْا لِمَ تَقُوْلُوْنَ مَا لَا تَفْعَلُوْنَ كَبُرَ مَقْتًا عِنْدَ اللهِ}$$
$$\text{أَنْ تَقُوْلُوْا مَالَا تَفْعَلُوْنَ}$$

"O believers! Why do you say what you do not do?
How despicable it is in the sight of Allah that
you say what you do not do!" [148]

---

[147] *Al-Aḥzāb*, 21.

[148] *Al-Ṣaff*, 2-3.

The Prophet Shuʿayb ﷺ also said to his people,

$$\text{وَمَا أُرِيدُ أَنْ أُخَالِفَكُمْ إِلَىٰ مَا أَنْهَاكُمْ عَنْهُ}$$

"I do not want to do what I am forbidding you from." [149]

He gave importance to his actions and speech being in conformity with each other.

We learn from this one of the fundamental principles of our religion: that we should concentrate on ourselves and our own faults more than those of others. Our Prophet ﷺ sternly warned us from the disease of focusing on and magnifying others' faults. This is because when you search for and magnify the mistakes of others, the deceitful Devil causes you to fall into the trap of thinking that you are better than others, which is not the quality of a true believer. Our Prophet ﷺ said,

$$\text{وَابْكِ عَلَى خَطِيئَتِكَ}$$

"Cry over your own mistakes."

Our own evil deeds should constantly reduce us to tears and busy us in repentance, let alone us having the time to prioritise the mistakes of others.

---

149 *Hūd*, 88.

Another extreme is a person having a notion that, "Because I am not perfect myself, I should not preach or advise anybody to do good". However, Allah ﷻ says,

كُنْتُمْ خَيْرَ أُمَّةٍ أُخْرِجَتْ لِلنَّاسِ تَأْمُرُونَ بِالْمَعْرُوفِ وَ تَنْهَوْنَ
عَنِ الْمُنْكَرِ وَتُؤْمِنُونَ بِاللهِ

"You are the best community ever raised for humanity—you encourage good, forbid evil, and believe in Allah. Had the People of the Book believed, it would have been better for them. Some of them are faithful, but most are rebellious." [150]

This verse explicitly mentions that the reason for us being the best nation is because we combine the qualities of commanding good, forbidding evil, and believing in Allah internally and externally. Thus, the verse of *Sūrah al-Ṣaff* is not to be used as an excuse for claiming that I should not enjoin good and forbid evil, as I am not perfect myself. Saʿīd ibn Jubayr ﷺ, the leading student of Ibn ʿAbbās ﷺ, once remarked,

"If perfection was a requirement before advising others, then every person would be silent as nobody is perfect."

The Qur'an does not say that you must be perfect before preaching, for no person can claim perfection. If this was

---

[150] *Āl ʿImrān*, 110.

the case, only the perfect Prophets could preach, and everybody else would have to remain silent. Rather, the Qur'an says that you should preach, but do not neglect or forget yourself. If an imperfect individual preaches to improve others with a conscience that acknowledges that he needs improvement himself, then this is in line with the Qur'anic injunction. Allah ﷻ clearly states the clause,

$$\text{وَتَنْسَوْنَ اَنْفُسَكُمْ}$$

"And fail to practice it yourselves"

This is where the sin lies—in failing to practice yourself.

Thus, it is very important for parents and elders of the community to be responsible and take care of those under their charge, even if they are not perfect and are committing sins themselves. We must certainly work on ourselves, but we must also try our best so that those who look up to us do not commit sins and take the wrong path. These two paths of improvement—personal and transitive—go hand in hand.

In summary, we should continue working on ourselves, acknowledging we are sinful, striving to achieve perfection, and feeling obligated to try our best to impact those in our immediate circle and to be positive role models for them. Never should we feel internally arrogant and presume that we have reached perfection, for this is what Allah ﷻ harshly criticises the Children of Israel for. This was when they began claiming that they are going to go to heaven exclusively and that they are the chosen ones, resulting in them sinfully criticising everyone else.

To conclude, we must be cautious of two extremes,

1. *The first extreme*—falling prey to arrogance and the devilish deception that we have attained salvation, resulting in us criticising everybody else.

2. *The opposite extreme*—the incorrect notion that until I become perfect I should not preach to others.

We should aim for personal perfection whilst also trying to become a role model for other people—that is the religion of Islam.

27

When Opposites Meet:
A Remarkable Aphorism Concerning the Law of Retaliation

In verse 179 of *Sūrah al-Baqarah*, another very powerful, common, and polysemic Arabic phrase is used. In this verse, Allah ﷻ says,

وَلَكُمْ فِي الْقِصَاصِ حَيٰوةٌ

"There is [security of] life for you in [the law of] retaliation..." [151]

The great linguist and scholar Imam al-Zamakhsharī comments on this passage by mentioning that it is one of the most powerful Qur'anic aphorisms. This is due to the mention of opposites within this single verse.

---

[151] *Al-Baqarah*, 179.

The word *qiṣāṣ* refers to the Islamic law of retaliation, in particular the death penalty. Allah ﷻ mentions that this law is inclusive of all, regardless of gender or societal status.

الْحُرُّ بِالْحُرِّ وَالْعَبْدُ بِالْعَبْدِ وَالْأُنْثَىٰ بِالْأُنْثَىٰ

"a free man for a free man, a slave for a slave, and a female for a female." [152]

In all cases, the murderer has the law of retaliation applied upon them, which was a new injunction introduced into society by Islam. In the pre-Islamic era, the affluent and those with noble lineage would be exempt from the laws of retaliation, whilst those of lower social standing would be readily handed over to be executed for the crime of murder. This unfair treatment would reach to such an extent that tribes would end up warring, yet still the noble or affluent would not be harmed or taken to task. Allah ﷻ wished to right this injustice, stipulating that the social status of a murderer shall not benefit them nor give them a hand above the law. The law should be equally applied to all, regardless of gender, affluence, nobility, or status. Allah ﷻ then says,

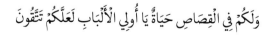

وَلَكُمْ فِي الْقِصَاصِ حَيَاةٌ يَا أُولِي الْأَلْبَابِ لَعَلَّكُمْ تَتَّقُونَ

---

[152] *Al-Baqarah*, 178.

"There is [security of] life for you in [the law of] retaliation [death penalty], O people of reason, so that you may become mindful [of Allah]." [153]

In this phenomenal verse, Allah ﷻ mentions and links the two opposites of life and death, by mentioning that the security of life lies with the death penalty.

A question may arise in regard to how this is possible, and what this Qur'anic statement is implying. First and foremost, as previously mentioned, in the pre-Islamic days of ignorance tribes would initiate lengthy warfare due to the refusal to hand over a socially noble or affluent murderer for punishment, thus causing many hundreds to die in lieu of this one murderer they originally refused to hand over. Based on this reality, the just law of equality revealed by Allah ﷻ allows many lives to be saved through one death penalty being exacted upon the socially noble or affluent murderer.

Another possible interpretation of this statement is that there is life for the murderer himself in the death penalty. Allah ﷻ has legislated these punishments to act as a *kaffārah* (expiation/atonement) of the sin committed. This way, the sinner may be absolved in the everlasting life of the Hereafter by repenting to Allah ﷻ and accepting the divinely legislated punishment. Our Prophet ﷺ said: "Whoever amongst you commits a crime and the [divinely legislated] punishment is

153 *Al-Baqarah*, 179.

exacted upon him, then it will be an expiation for him." So, if the murderer repents and the law of retaliation is exacted, he will attain salvation from that sin in the eternal life of the Hereafter. However, if he does not, Allah ﷻ informs us,

$$\text{وَمَن يَقْتُلْ مُؤْمِنًا مُّتَعَمِّدًا فَجَزَآؤُهُ جَهَنَّمُ خَٰلِدًا فِيهَا}$$

"And whoever kills a believer intentionally, their reward will be Hell—where they will stay indefinitely." [154]

The third possible interpretation is that 'life' refers to the life of society. When the act of murder is emphatically criminalised to such an extent that it becomes common knowledge that a murderer will be executed, this will serve as an extremely effective deterrent. Also, through the penalty being exacted on a small scale, society will be saved from any such odious murderers who still dare commit this heinous crime despite the stern warnings. Thus, the law of retaliation is a great aid in upholding the sanctity of life.

We learn from these explanations that the laws of the Shariah (Islamic laws) have been divinely legislated in order to protect human society and aid it in flourishing. The laws are not meant to make life difficult, nor are they archaic or barbaric as some uninformed critics allege. In fact, they are much to the contrary, for the Islamic laws are the most conducive to the physical and spiritual welfare of all societies.

---

[154] *Al-Nisā'*, 93.

If we look towards the penal system of the Western world, it is one of the largest disasters of humanity. If we look at incarceration rates, America has one of the highest in the world. In fact, one out of four people in prison are in America; in other words, if you add up all the prisoners of the world, one-fourth of them are in America and the other three-fourths are divided amongst the remaining two hundred plus countries of the world. We are also aware that prisons are for-profit organisations. We also know that a person charged with first-degree murder typically receives life imprisonment without the possibility of parole. What is the benefit of taking a person and jailing them for 60 to 70 years, particularly if they are a young offender? The jailed individual does not benefit from this, nor does his family, and in the majority of scenarios, they will not be rehabilitated effectively in this lengthy period. When they are eventually released, they have no direction in life and are prone to re-offend. Bearing this in mind, what is the purpose of taking a normal healthy human being and locking him up in jail for such a long period of time? The prisoners are treated no better than animals. In fact, if we were to lock an animal up in a similar manner, we may be put in jail ourselves. This is the clear failure of the prison system.

On the other hand, the Shariah system is a holistic and perfect system. The Shariah does not dictate that all criminals are indefinitely locked up in cells, for this only makes the criminal, the environment, his family and his children suffer, harming and breaking the building blocks of society and serving no long-term benefit. Rather, Allah ﷻ tells us that in

the divinely legislated laws there is life for you. If someone is guilty of a crime, exact the legislated punishment upon them, and move on after having made a firm public statement and putting in place an effective deterrent, which is one of the purposes of the Shariah laws along with rehabilitation. Allah ﷻ explicitly mentions in *Sūrah al-Nūr*,

$$وَلْيَشْهَدْ عَذَابَهُمَا طَائِفَةٌ مِّنَ الْمُؤْمِنِينَ$$

"And let a number of believers witness their punishment." [155]

This is as witnessing the punishment will deter potential criminals from crossing certain limits and red lines. Towards the end of the verse of retaliation, Allah ﷻ says,

$$يَا أُولِي الْأَلْبَابِ لَعَلَّكُمْ تَتَّقُونَ$$

"O people of reason, so that you may become mindful [of Allah]"

This indicates to us that we need to ponder and think about the wisdom of divine legislation. We should not cower to the censure of outsiders and critics, who falsely claim that 'Islam is backwards'. Such a fallacious statement is based on their own ignorance and lack of study, for our Shariah makes complete sense to any fair-minded individual who honestly researches and investigates. By doing so, Allah ﷻ says that "you may become mindful [of Allah]."

---

[155] *Al-Nūr*, 2.

28

The Positive
Affirmation of Faith
Through Observation

The next verse we will be exploring contains a beautiful aphorism from which multiple benefits can be derived. The aphorism we will be exploring is found in verse 260 of *Sūrah al-Baqarah*, where the Qur'an states,

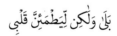

"Yes I do, but just so my heart can be reassured."[156]

The context of this verse is in relation to Ibrāhīm 🕊 and his dispute with the evil king Nimrūd regarding the identity of the true Lord. Nimrūd had arrogantly claimed lordship for himself, so Ibrāhīm 🕊 boldly rejected this claim and told him that my Lord Allah 🕊 is the only one who causes

THE PARABLES OF THE QUR'AN

---

156 *Al-Baqarah*, 260.

death and can bring the dead back to life. When Ibrāhīm ﷺ was later away from Nimrūd in seclusion, he asked Allah, 'My Lord! Show me how you give life to the dead.' Allah ﷻ replied, 'Do you not have faith [that I can resurrect the dead]?' It is then that Ibrāhīm ﷺ made the famous statement,

$$بَلَىٰ وَلَٰكِن لِّيَطْمَئِنَّ قَلْبِي$$

"Yes I do, but just so my heart can be reassured."[157]

Ibrahim ﷺ already had faith and believed in the proof beforehand, but he was still asking Allah ﷻ to show him the proof. This is as he just wanted his heart to be steadfast, secure, firm, and at complete ease. This makes this aphorism a very powerful phrase.

Humankind has been created weak, such that hearing of something does somewhat satisfy us. But only by physically seeing something do we attain complete satisfaction. In English, it is commonly said that 'seeing is believing'. This is a reality, for the power of visuals in the human epistemological framework is greater than the power of speech. The Prophet ﷺ is reported to have said in a Hadith,

$$لَيْسَ الْخَبَرُ كَالْمُعَايَنَةِ$$

"[Receiving] information is not like witnessing."

---

[157] *Al-Baqarah*, 260.

This principle has been manifested in an incident from the wonderful life of Mūsā ﷺ. On one occasion, Mūsā ﷺ was speaking to Allah ﷻ directly with no intermediary on Mount Sinai, as Allah ﷻ mentions,

$$\text{وَكَلَّمَ اللهُ مُوسَى تَكْلِيمًا}$$

"And to Mūsā Allah spoke directly."[158]

Allah ﷻ says to him that his people have worshipped the calf. Upon this, Mūsā ﷺ becomes angry and returns to his people,

$$\text{فَرَجَعَ مُوسَى إِلَى قَوْمِهِ غَضْبَانَ أَسِفًا}$$

"So Mūsā returned to his people, furious and sorrowful."[159]

Now, when he sees the calf and the people foolishly worshipping it, what was his reaction? He already knew that they were doing so, as Allah ﷻ had previously informed him. However, when he sees it with his own eyes, his anger intensifies. Our scholars say that it intensified to such an extent that he threw the Divine Tablets and broke them!

These tablets were of great honour and value, being divine revelation from Allah ﷻ similar to the Noble Qur'an. It is extremely important that such divine words are respected.

---

[158] *Al-Nisā'*, 164.

[159] *Ṭā Hā*, 86.

However, Mūsā ﷺ was so furious upon seeing what his people had done that he threw and broke the Divine Tablets, only picking them up later.

وَأَلْقَى ٱلْأَلْوَاحَ وَأَخَذَ بِرَأْسِ أَخِيهِ يَجُرُّهُۥ إِلَيْهِ

"Then he threw down the Tablets and grabbed his brother by the hair, dragging him closer."[160]

He then grabbed his brother, interrogating him on how he dared to let the people do what they had done. We learn from this incident and the reaction of Mūsā ﷺ that being informed of something is certainly not the same as visually witnessing it.

Returning to the story of Ibrāhīm ﷺ and his request to see proof of the dead being resurrected, Allah ﷻ decided to show him such proof,

قَالَ فَخُذْ أَرْبَعَةً مِّنَ ٱلطَّيْرِ فَصُرْهُنَّ إِلَيْكَ ثُمَّ ٱجْعَلْ عَلَىٰ كُلِّ جَبَلٍ مِّنْهُنَّ جُزْءًا ثُمَّ ٱدْعُهُنَّ يَأْتِينَكَ سَعْيًا ۚ وَٱعْلَمْ أَنَّ ٱللَّهَ عَزِيزٌ حَكِيمٌ

"Allah said, 'Then bring four birds, train them to come to you, [then cut them into pieces] and scatter them on different hilltops. Then call them back, they will fly to you in haste. And [so you will] know that Allah is Almighty, All-Wise.'"[161]

---

[160] *Al-Aʿrāf*, 150.

[161] *Al-Baqarah*, 260.

We also learn from this incident that faith is of levels (*darajāt*). A person can always increase in the levels of their faith. Even the Prophets such as Ibrāhīm ﷺ wished to increase their faith, despite already being at lofty stations. We can also increase our faith by connecting with Allah, attentively listening to and reflecting on the Qur'an, and by increasing our beneficial knowledge.

The final point of this chapter is one of extreme sensitivity and importance, particularly for the younger generation. When you have questions about faith and religion, there is nothing wrong with asking for some evidence. It is completely acceptable to confess belief, but still try to understand why. There may be certain aspects of faith, commandments, and verses of the Qur'an that perhaps you or I do not understand. It is okay to question and search for answers, as long as it is done with the correct mentality and mindset. If our questioning is in order to arrogantly challenge Allah ﷻ, that is disbelief and blameworthy. However, if we are questioning in order to try and understand the religion by approaching the right people, this is not blameworthy. We learn this from the excellent example of Ibrāhīm ﷺ. When he stood before the evil king Nimrūd, he vehemently defended *tawḥīd*. Yet when he was later before Allah ﷻ in seclusion, he genuinely requested some affirmation despite already having firm faith.

The lesson we derive from this is that it is permissible to ask legitimate questions. In order to find the answer to these questions, do not approach Nimrūd and the arrogant followers of Nimrūd—those who stubbornly reject the truth. Rather, we should approach the people of firm knowledge.

$$\text{فَاسْأَلُوا أَهْلَ الذِّكْرِ إِن كُنتُمْ لَا تَعْلَمُونَ}$$

"You [people] can ask those who have knowledge if you do not know."[162]

We should not problematise approaching the people of knowledge. Come with a heart full of faith to the people of faith, and after clarifying that you do sincerely believe, ask them to explain to you these matters and help you understand. If we take this approach and go to the right people with the right heart, we will find whatever answers we require and our faith will also increase. This is the reality of our faith and the excellent example that was provided to us by Ibrāhīm 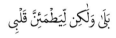.

May Allah ﷻ make us amongst those who say,

$$\text{بَلَىٰ وَلَٰكِن لِّيَطْمَئِنَّ قَلْبِي}$$

"Yes I do, but just so my heart can be reassured."[163]

---

[162] *Al-Naḥl*, 43.

[163] *Al-Baqarah*, 260.

We conclude by praying that Allah 🕮 makes us amongst,

وَالذَّاكِرِينَ اللَّهَ كَثِيرًا وَالذَّاكِرَاتِ

"Men and women who remember Allah often." [164]

May Allah forgive all our sins, exalt our ranks, and make us amongst,

ٱلَّذِينَ يَسْتَمِعُونَ ٱلْقَوْلَ فَيَتَّبِعُونَ أَحْسَنَهُۥ ۚ أُوْلَٰٓئِكَ ٱلَّذِينَ هَدَىٰهُمُ ٱللَّهُ وَأُوْلَٰٓئِكَ هُمْ أُوْلُواْ ٱلْأَلْبَٰبِ

"Those who listen to what is said and follow the best of it, they are the ones Allah has guided, and they are people of understanding." [165]

We proclaim that if there was any benefit in these words, this is all from Allah 🕮 and His blessings. We seek Allah's 🕮 forgiveness if any mistake has been made, for it is surely from myself and the whisperings of the Devil. Allah 🕮 and His Messenger 🕮 are free of my mistakes.

May Allah 🕮 reward you all immensely.

THE PARABLES OF THE QUR'AN

210

---

[164] *Al-Aḥzāb*, 35.

[165] *Al-Zumar*, 18.